THE PRICE
OF
PROSPERITY

*A Realistic Appraisal of the
Future of Our
National Economy*

Peter L. Bernstein

D0064507

WILEY

John Wiley & Sons, Inc.

Published by John Wiley & Sons, Inc., Hoboken, New Jersey.
Published simultaneously in Canada.
Originally published by Random House, Inc. in 1962.

For general information on our other products and services or for technical support,
please contact our Customer Care Department within the United States at (800)
762-2974, outside the United States at (317) 572-3993 or fax (317) 572-4002.

Wiley also publishes its books in a variety of electronic formats. Some content that
appears in print may not be available in electronic books. For more information about
Wiley products, visit our web site at www.wiley.com.

Library of Congress Cataloging-in-Publication Data:

Bernstein, Peter L.
    The price of prosperity : a realistic appraisal of the future of our national economy/
Peter L. Bernstein ; foreword by Paul A. Samuelson.
        p.   cm.
    Includes bibliographical references and index.
    ISBN 978-0-470-28757-6 (pbk.)
        1. Full employment policies—United States.   2. Economic forecasting—
United States.   3. United States—Economic policy.   I. Title.
HC106.5.B46 2008
330.973—dc22
                                                                            2008028074

Printed in the United States of America
10 9 8 7 6 5 4 3 2 1

THE PRICE
OF
PROSPERITY

To Shirley,
with love

CONTENTS

Foreword by Paul A. Samuelson   ix

New Introduction   xiii

Original Preface   xxv

Chapter 1   The Arithmetic of Optimism   1

Chapter 2   The Burden of Government   18

Chapter 3   The Fear of Taxes   36

Chapter 4   The Uses of Government   56

Chapter 5   The Tragedy of Errors   78

Chapter 6   The Economics of Democracy   98

Statistical Appendix   121

Acknowledgments   131

Notes   133

Index   137

FOREWORD

Economic historians can benefit from reading and comparing Peter Bernstein's successive books on American and global economic trends and ideas.

In particular, his *The Price of Prosperity* came just at the time in the 1960s when the Roosevelt-Kennedy-Johnson paradigms were harvesting the fruits of the new scientific findings of macroeconomics.

It was a time of earned optimism. Maybe with optimism comes complacency. No one in the 1960s realized at the time that America and the world economy were then at a fork in the road. Fable has it that baseball's sage Yogi Berra said, "When you come to a fork in the road, take it."

Nature's unmanicured jungle provides no recognizable forks in the road. The same holds for realistic dynamic economic history. In lively, understandable prose, author Bernstein made clear that there are no free lunches. Needed valuable public services are in tradeoff with private consumption, always. As Justice Oliver Holmes famously said, "Taxes are the price we pay for civilization."

What no one realized in the mid-1960s was that the quagmire of the Vietnam war—which Eisenhower-Dulles passed on to Kennedy and Johnson, and which they passed on to the Nixon-Kissinger-Burns trio—sent the American electorate off in a new libertarian course.

Jotting down counterfactual economic history cannot erase actual subsequent history. But it can teach useful lessons.

To sustain the singular growth dynamic of Camelot, after America had cut its losses in Indochina, optimal macro policy would have had to recognize that miracle growth in competing emerging societies—in Japan, Hong Kong, South Korea, Taiwan, and Singapore—did require a sizeable devaluation of the dollar.

Paranoid President Nixon, along with his shenanigan Watergate manipulators and with concurrence from his complaisant Federal Reserve Chairman Arthur Burns, did abandon Bretton Woods dollar parities. But at the same time, under reelection anxieties, Nixon introduced the price and wage controls that would plague the stagflation supply-shock economy of the 1970s.

No longer centrist macro and micro prudence, the radical right supply-side follies of the Reagan era took front stage. As economic law predicted, the 1914 to 1985 U.S. pattern of being a *creditor* nation reversed itself quickly during the Reagan years.

Thus, the work of a canny Bernstein is never done. Sufficient to each day was Bernstein's vision of middle-of-the-road money and fiscal programs. The libertarians were at the gate. And the melodrama still goes on in this era of American trade deficits and deliberate destruction of the nation's tax base.

—Paul A. Samuelson

NEW
INTRODUCTION

The *Price of Prosperity* was my first book. It has always had a special place in my heart. Moreover, the whole project came into being as a result of a sudden and unplanned sequence of events.

One day in 1959, an editor at the *New York Times* called and invited me to write a short piece about the lore of gold for the magazine section. He had seen something I had written elsewhere and thought I had some promise as a writer. Not long after, a senior editor at Doubleday named Sam Vaughan called me to say he had seen the article in the *Times* and urged me to start work on a book.

I had been pondering for a long time the problem of how the economy could grow fast enough to provide jobs for the swarm of baby boomers when they started to reach working age at the end of the 1960s. When I suggested that topic to Sam Vaughan, he was enthusiastic and encouraged me to go ahead and get started.

Then Sam gave me some editorial advice I have never forgotten: "This is going to be your first book, and I can tell you that writing books is nothing like writing an article. With an article, you know you have limited space. In addition, articles compete with other articles for the reader's attention. But when somebody buys your book, they buy it because they want to read it. You have their attention. So use the space freely. You have no need to be counting words or pages. You can feel free to digress and give it all you've got."

The Price of Prosperity hit the bookstores in the spring of 1962. On publication date, my wife and I went out to celebrate with lunch at a fancy restaurant, including the appropriate number of martinis to match the occasion. Easter was about ten days off, and, on the way home, we saw a grey-and-white rabbit in a pet shop. We were in such a jolly mood we walked into the pet shop, bought the rabbit, and took him home. We named him Prospero, after *The Price of Prosperity*. Prospero was the first in a long line of pet rabbits who graced our lives over many years.

New Introduction

This book has also inspired its own line of descendants, each of which has brought its own special flavor of joy and excitement. Nine more books have followed *The Price of Prosperity*, including two co-authored with my late and beloved friend Robert Heilbroner.

The primary message of *The Price of Prosperity* is in the profound difference between projections and forecasts. We can put together all kinds of statistical material from the past to describe the future. If we are gloom-mongers, we produce projections of disastrous scenarios. If we are incurable optimists, we can paint beautiful pictures of a glorious future. All we have to do is choose the desired set of historical statistics and get to work.

The Price of Prosperity refers to this process as economic arithmetic. The book's mission is to test out the necessary conditions for the fulfillment of the wildly optimistic long-run projections that were popular in 1960 to 1961 when I was writing the book. Based on economic arithmetic, these projections combined firm expectations for sharply improving labor productivity with the impending accelerated growth in the labor force as the baby boomers reached working age. The result of these calculations was a glittering promise of higher living standards by the mid-1970s.

The search for the necessary conditions to make those dreams come true was not an easy one. At that moment, the baby boomers were still too young to be entering the labor force. The oldest were in their mid-teens. The cohort received plenty of attention nevertheless, as all groups of young people receive attention, caused primarily by their social behavior and the strain they impose on their parents' pocketbook. But nobody appeared to be worrying about what would happen when the baby boomers would be old enough to enter the labor force and start looking for jobs. On the contrary, most people figured it would be a relief not to have so many young people acting up, to say nothing of the pleasure of getting them off the family payroll.

People do not land jobs just because they are in the job market. Employment expands when the demand for goods and services expands. That condition is never pre-ordained. The problem, then, was as simple as its solution was complex. Sustaining a low level of unemployment as the baby boomers matured would require unprecedented peacetime growth in the demand for goods and services. Demand for higher living standards is always there, but these projections ignored any problems that might arise in generating sufficient incomes to pay for that big jump in the consumption of goods and services. The whole exercise was meaningless unless we could identify the sources of growth in purchasing power.

In 1960, the number of people of working age—say, ages 20 to 64—was 94 million, just about half the total population.* Ten years earlier, the working age population had been 89 million. Thus, the number of people of working age had increased only about 5 percent since 1950, compared with the growth of nearly 20 percent in the total population. Under those conditions, sustaining full employment in most years was no problem.

But by the end of the 1960s, the oldest of the baby boomers would begin seeking jobs and that number would grow at an accelerating rate. By 1980, the cohort aged 20 to 64 would grow to about 130 million, an increase of 43 percent from 1960, while the total population would increase by only 25 percent. It was clear that a rapid expansion in the demand for goods and services would be essential if the country were to achieve full employment over that twenty-year span.

After a detailed exploration of the alternatives, I could find no solution to this problem other than an increase in government spending (state and local as well as federal) relative to the economy as a whole. The private sector by

---

* In the book, I measure working age from 14 to 64, but the breakdowns of the demographic data today are different from what they were over forty years ago. The story, however, is the same. As I write on page 7, "The increase in the number of people of working age from 1965 to 1970 will be as great as the entire increase from 1947 to 1957; the growth after 1970 will be at an even faster rate than during the 1960s."

itself did not appear likely to provide a sufficient growth in demand.

The remainder of the book is a critical examination of all the issues surrounding government spending. I tried to think of every possible argument against government spending and then proceeded to show why those arguments, one after another, would not hold water. Indeed, as the argument progressed, I became increasingly convinced there were strong positive reasons for providing for an increase in government expenditure.

The difficulty in reaching full employment I identified in 1961 did develop as I had feared. During the 1960s, when the baby boomers were still in diapers or in school, everything had been great. An average of 3.5 million people were unemployed, equal to 4.8 percent of the labor force. At the end of the decade, the unemployment rate was down to 3.5 percent, close to a practical minimum. But in the 1970s, thanks to the bulging influx of baby boomers seeking jobs, the level of output and employment turned out to be far below what the economic arithmetic had projected. From 1970 to 1974, unemployment averaged 5.4 percent; the average over the next five years was 7.0 percent in a range of 5.8 percent to 7.7 percent—eight million people at the worst, or just about the same number as were unemployed at the time of Pearl Harbor when the economy was still showing the consequences of the Great Depression.[*]

Economic conditions during the 1970s are usually referred to as "stagflation," or a combination of stagnation and inflation. Inflation there was for certain: from the end of 1969 to the end of 1979, the Cost of Living Index rose at an annual rate of 7.4 percent One reason for this dire outcome was Federal Reserve policy. The members of the Open Market Committee were reluctant to make money sufficiently tight to snuff out inflation at a time of unprecedented growth in the labor force. Stagnation, however, is something of a misnomer. The economy grew, in real terms, at an annual rate of 3.3 percent over the decade of the 1970s, not far below the average of 3.8 percent for all ten-year periods ending 1957 through 1969—but average growth was insufficient to create full employment at a time when the increase in the labor force was rapidly accelerating. In addition, the widely anticipated rise in productivity failed to make an appearance. Productivity growth for the decade was only 2.6 percent a year.

---

[*] The arrival of the baby boomers into the labor force drove the median age of the labor force from 39 years in 1970 down to only 34½ years in 1980; their aging since then has pushed it back up to about 41½.

Perhaps the poor record on unemployment reflected the failure of the nation to provide the increase in government spending I had called for in *The Price of Prosperity.* Measured by government purchases of goods and services, including state and local spending (the metric I use in the book to exclude transfer payments like social security and unemployment insurance), government accounted for 21 percent of gross national product in 1962, the year the book came out. In 1979, even with defense spending on a steep uptrend, total government purchases were still 20 percent of gross national product.[*]

The Price of Prosperity is a paean for government spending. In a romantic kind of way, the book analyzes the many positives government can contribute. The merits of government spending, which I refer to on page 66, in the chapter on "The Uses of Government," include "education, better roads, urban renewal, less juvenile delinquency, better-balanced defense programs, less poverty in foreign lands, and so on and on and on." Then I add, "[W]here there are needs that a profit-oriented economy will fail to meet, [there] is no reason to argue that such needs have

---

[*] This ratio was around 22 percent in the early 1980s but has declined gradually since then. At the latest readings, government purchases were 17.5 percent of what is now known as gross domestic product.

a second-class character whose satisfaction can readily be postponed."

Four and a half decades later a profound change has taken place in my view of these matters. This shift has two sources. One is subjective but the other confronts hard facts that make a radical difference from conditions in the early 1960s.

First, I have my doubts that what I wrote about government spending in the early 1960s is a satisfactory description of government spending in our own time. Although all of those laudatory objectives listed above are included in government today, unfortunately a lot more goes on in Washington and the state capitals that I would just as happily exclude. Graft and waste were always present, but now they occur on a larger scale than in the early 1960s and in a balder and less apologetic fashion as well. Defense spending back then was minimal; today it is a critical variable in the size and objectives of the federal sector. In short, the romance with which I once embraced the notion of government spending has been replaced to a significant degree with something more sullied.

Second, and less debatable, the baby boomers have come a long way since I wrote this book. Then they were still in their teens, at the very edge of joining the labor force and seeking employment. Now they are graying men and women on the crest of retirement, with some forty years of employment behind them. Back then, the problem was one of trying to find jobs for all of them. Today, the problem will be one of trying to finance the promises for retirement and health care the taxpayers have bestowed upon them. Unlike the economic arithmetic of which I was so skeptical in 1962, today's projections are to be taken seriously: a huge mandated increase in government spending lies ahead and threatens to crowd out a host of other urgent needs in the public sector. That threat will be real unless difficult and painful adjustments are made in the promises the government is expected to keep.

Some 75 million people—a quarter of the total population—are in the age group 45 to 64 and will turn 65 over the next fifteen years. The 45 to 64 age group has more than doubled since I wrote *The Price of Prosperity* in 1960 to 1961, while the total population has increased by only 67 percent. This is a problem to worry about!

Thus, I end this introduction on a note of irony. One of the surprises to me when I wrote *The Price of Prosperity* was the absence of concern over what would happen in the labor market when the baby boomers reached working age. Nobody seemed to be worrying about them. Everything would turn out all right.

The situation today is exactly the opposite. Now people do worry about what is going to happen in the

American economy when the baby boomers reach retirement age.

At long last, the futures of the baby boomers are receiving the national attention they deserved when I was writing *The Price of Prosperity*.

ORIGINAL PREFACE

The preparation of revised editions always opens the author to the temptation of using hindsight to make him appear wiser and more prescient than he had been when the original edition appeared. Despite the passage of five years and some major changes in economic thinking, I have resisted this temptation here. The argument reflects no changes in substance whatsoever, although the statistics that appear in the last four chapters have been updated where appropriate.

Hindsight has led me to yield to one temptation, however, which is to improve the readability of the early part of the book. Hence, the first five chapters have been condensed into one, thereby eliminating much discussion that the passage of time has made superfluous. In addition, the statistical analysis in the original five chapters now appears unnecessarily tedious and has been relegated in this edition to an appendix.

I am happy to have this opportunity to express once again my gratitude to those whose help I have acknowledged on a later page and to express as well my thanks for invaluable editorial guidance from Mrs. Miriam Z. Klipper of Random House.

—Peter L. Bernstein
Brattleboro, Vermont
April 1966

THE PRICE
OF
PROSPERITY

Chapter 1

THE ARITHMETIC OF OPTIMISM

In real life, you have first of all to find the question; to learn to identify, almost as if by instinct, the one forgery amongst a mass of genuine signatures, or to spot the googly amongst a string of innocent leg breaks.
—Speech by MR. ANTHONY TUKE
Chairman of Barclays Bank, London

1.

While it is far easier to describe Heaven than it is to provide a map showing how to get there, the man who undertakes the first without considering the second has done us little service. Yet the economists who purvey the glowing and finely detailed descriptions of the prosperity of the years ahead may have failed us on just this count.

Of course we face a dazzling opportunity. Our labor force is on the verge of an enormous expansion. Automation is rapidly increasing our ability to produce more goods with less work. Our economic history has been characterized by the happy combination of bold businessmen and ingenious engineers. Within the entire scope of our economy, from private houses to public works, we stand a real chance of stamping out want in the United States during the decade of the 1970s.

But we lack the directions to find our way to this economic paradise. Output and employment do not rise simply because men are looking for jobs or hungry mouths want to be filled. If this were so, we would never have unemployment, and poverty might long since have disappeared. This is, in fact, the central question to which this book is addressed: since the number of Americans seeking work in the decade ahead is going to increase more than half again as rapidly as during the years since the end of World War II, can we in fact make the adjustments necessary to create so many additional jobs? And what happens if we fail?

We must therefore begin with the recognition that the exciting forecasts of the late 1960s and the 1970s are not forecasts at all, even though they have every outward appearance of things to come. They are nothing more than real estate brochures about Heaven, based upon the assumption that somehow we will wind up there. They are economic arithmetic, which is not yet a substitute for economic analysis. As a presentation of goals or potentials, they are useful; as indications of what *will* be, they are positively dangerous.

They are dangerous because they are based on the assumption that what has been will continue to be. Yet the ocean floors of history are littered with the hulks of economic predictions that never made the far shore— floating hopes that foundered because they were navigated under this false assumption. Belief in an everlasting prosperity contributed to the smash that hit us at the end of the 1920s. Assurance of a never-ending stagnation prolonged the depression—and then led to the erroneous expectation that the end of World War II would signify the immediate return of the deeply depressed conditions of the 1930s. It is difficult to remember now, but the inflationary avalanche of 1946 to 1948 was in large part intensified by policies that were based upon this incorrect extrapolation into the future.

It is amazing how frequently we have to learn—and how frequently we forget—that each age has its own peculiarities, its unique character. But that is probably because men hate change and are reluctant to accept its inevitability.

2.

Those who merely multiply the greatly increased number of potential workers by another greatly increased estimate for output per man-hour can indeed come up with some dazzling possibilities for the years ahead.

But these arithmetic optimists have fallen into this tempting thought: because the number of potential workers will rise at an increasingly rapid rate in the coming decade and beyond, employment and incomes will expand; because employment and incomes will be high, demand will run strong; because demand will run strong, employment and income will be high. But in such circular logic, there is only *one* behavioral term: demand. Hence, we must first question how and why demand will rise. Without expanding demand, businessmen will refuse to raise their production schedules or to hire new workers; without rising production and employment, we have no economic growth. Demand, therefore, is the keystone of the whole structure upon which our projections of the future must be built.

In finding the path to full employment during a period when the number of workers is expanding more rapidly than in the past, we must begin with the recognition that economic analysis is meaningless if it ignores the dynamics of demand. Economics is more flesh and blood than mere arithmetic calculations, more a study of society than of technology. Physical facts—even those of the greatest economic importance, such as population structure, raw material supplies, and the character of technological progress—have meaning to the economist only as a backdrop against which human desires and decisions perform.

Economic growth, in short, is never guaranteed. Even if the capacity to produce expands, we have no assurance that demand will rise fast enough to absorb the additional output that can be produced. Indeed, expansion is usually undertaken only in response to signs of rising demand. But this means, in turn, that, if the demands of consumers and businessmen fail to increase fast enough to keep step with our productive capacities, the only way slow growth and unemployment can be avoided is through an accelerated increase in the quantity of our output that is purchased by the government.

This suggests that, under certain conditions, an increase in governmental activities might actually *stimulate* growth; this is a fundamental difference in emphasis from the widely held idea that they may be a burden more easily met if supported by an economy with a rising level of production. We might in fact test the proposition that government would have to be the support rather than the burden of an expanding economy, that our living standards might be higher with it than without it. We shall examine this possibility extensively in the chapters that follow.

3.

While our analysis of the future cannot avoid taking off from an understanding of the past, a tedious review of our postwar economic history would serve little purpose at this point. Yet we would do well to remember that the past twenty-odd years have been marked by persistent change, usually in unexpected directions or in magnitudes that came as a surprise to most of us. The wide variety of economic experience we have known since the war is, then, a warning that the past is a most treacherous basis upon which to predict the future.

Nevertheless, if we study carefully all of the statistics, all of the events, all of the forces at work in the postwar years, we do find one strategic factor that was relatively constant during the 1940s and 1950s, that began to change only in the mid-1960s, and that will be entirely different in the 1970s. Furthermore, this factor emerged from a set of paradoxes. Although something new, its origin reached back to the period after World War I. Although man-made, it was inevitable. Although its ultimate influence was to create highly stimulating expectations, this new factor was itself the consequence of a less buoyant view of what the future might hold.

The factor to which I refer is the relative shortage of labor that characterized the postwar years and was in turn the consequence of the downward plunge in American birth rates that began at the end of World War I and deepened dramatically during the depression. Coming at the same time as the postwar boom, this strange quirk in our population structure had a critical impact on wage levels, business investment, and consumer behavior.

The figures are striking. During the 1930s, the number of children and teenagers actually declined. But during the decade of the 1940s, they increased by 6.2 million and then by another 18.4 million during the 1950s. Meanwhile, the 20 to 24 age group showed virtually no change at all from 1940 to 1960 and the 25 to 34 group registered only a nominal rise. If we assume that the labor force is drawn from those people aged 14 to 64, we find that this group rose by less than ten million during the first ten years after the war and shrank from 66.5 percent of the total population to less than 61 percent.

But now this situation is changing rapidly. The increase in the number of people of working age from 1965 to 1970 will be as great as the entire increase from 1947 to 1957; the growth after 1970 will be at an even faster rate than during the 1960s. This means that, while we have become adjusted to the dearth of young workers that resulted from the post–World War I birthrate patterns, we must now seek an entirely new set of adjustments as we move into the years that will be influenced by the reversal of these patterns after World War II.

These figures also raise some other intriguing questions about the impact of population trends on the level of business activity. For example, the arithmetic optimists point to the increasingly rapid growth in the labor force as their key argument for a booming prosperity; they sweeten their case further by predicting that the growth in the number of young adults will swell the number of marriages and household formations and thereby greatly stimulate the demand for goods and services.

Unfortunately, economic behavior is more complicated than that. We are just not able to set a crude equation between an expansion in the labor force and a rise in the level of production. Thus, the increase in the 20 to 34 age group during the 1930s was about the same as during the 1920s and much greater than during the 1950s. Can the arithmetic optimists tell us, then, why economic growth during the 1930s was so much slower than during the 1920s? Indeed, if we follow their reasoning to its logical conclusion and argue that prosperity depends primarily upon a high marriage and household formation rate, then we should have had a deep depression during the 1950s, when the number of young adults and the number of marriages were actually declining!

These observations tell us that we can find no simple link here between cause and effect. Thus, if the number of people of working age grows more slowly than the rest of the population, we can have no assurance that we will have a repetition of the great postwar business boom (any more than a rapidly expanding labor force can promise rapid economic growth). In fact, if the relative shortage of labor leads to wage increases that depress profit margins—as classical economic theory would lead us to expect—businessmen may become discouraged and unemployment and depression will result.

The interesting aspect of the postwar period is that the traditionally depressing effect of rising real wages was reversed during these years into a powerfully favorable influence on the economy, despite widespread and vocal complaints about the damage we were supposedly suffering from the wage-price spiral. On the one hand, business firms were induced to spend large sums on plant and equipment to economize on labor, the scarce and expensive factor of production. At the same time, the enjoyment of rising dollar incomes and the assurance that jobs were relatively easy to find created a free-spending and free-borrowing attitude among consumers; personal expenditures were a sturdy prop to the economy long after the first wave of pent-up postwar demands was satisfied and even though the typically highest-spending age groups lagged in number behind the rest of the population.

The powerful forward impetus of consumer spending is undoubtedly familiar; the impact of these trends on investment is worth spelling out. From 1947 to 1965, for example, modernization of plant and equipment and development of new products and new techniques of production led to an increase in total physical output that was nearly four times as fast as the increase in the number of people employed, while the number of hours worked declined at the same time. This is in contrast to the period from 1929 to 1947, when output increased only two and a half times as fast as employment.

These forces may be seen from another even more meaningful angle. One of the characteristic features of American economic history has been to increase the use of capital goods faster than we have expanded the use of labor: we are a capitalistic economy in a very real sense of the word. During the postwar years, however, this tendency was greatly accelerated to triple the long-term relationship between the increase in capital goods and the increase in labor.[1]

4.

If we attempt to apply all of this to a forecast of what the level of output and employment will be in 1970 or 1975, we may fairly ask—as the arithmetic optimists fail to ask—whether the shift from labor shortage to a much more ample labor supply will in fact dampen or even eliminate the stimuli the economy enjoyed through the free-spending attitudes of consumers and the urgency of businessmen to substitute machines for workers.

Indeed, in making our forecast, we have only one sure fact on which to base our estimates: the number of people of working age is going to increase much more rapidly in the future than it has in the past. But what proportion of the people of working age will actually seek jobs? How many of those seeking work will find it? How many hours a week will they work? How much will each of them be able to produce in an hour's or a week's work? We have no answer to these questions—only guesses.

Nevertheless, because of the acceleration in the growth of the labor force, the increasing attractiveness of work to married women, and the technological advances that are becoming commonplace in our time, even conservative responses to these questions can yield dramatic results to the arithmetic they imply. Nothing extravagant in the way of assumptions is required to conclude that our total output between 1965 and 1975 could increase faster than during the great postwar upsurge of 1947 to 1957 or in the powerful boom years that followed 1960. Remember—these are potentials rather than predictions, but the potentials are indeed impressive. They indicate, in short, that by 1975 we could be producing three times as much as we were able to produce when World War II came to an end, which works out to a tripling of output in about thirty years during which the population rose by less than fifty percent. In plain English, this means that the affluent society is within reach of reality.

If we are to achieve this objective, however, our discussion up to this point suggests that we must find favorable answers to two basic questions:

First, will the environment be congenial to such a rapid rate of growth in our capacity to produce? That is, will the labor force grow as fast and will the improvement in productivity be as great as these projections assume? If the assumptions are too optimistic, the physical and technical conditions that permit major economic growth will fall short.

Second, even if the physical *capacity* for production expands rapidly, will the dynamics of the years in which labor was in short supply persist to such a degree that the *demand* for goods and services will increase just as rapidly or more rapidly when the supply of labor is expanding at an accelerated rate?

The answer to the first question is a hopeful one. History does show that the American economy is capable of achieving rapid rates of growth in output when called upon to do so by a burgeoning expansion in demand.[2] Indeed, except for very brief periods of time—one or two years at the most—our capacity to produce typically outruns demand by enough of a margin so that it is unlikely to be a limiting factor: it accommodates itself adequately to the growth in demand.

This means that we must continue to put our emphasis on the answer to the second question—the outlook for demand, the truly significant factor. But the prediction of demand, which depends upon behavioral and psychological considerations as well as economic ones, is much more difficult than the prediction of supply, which is primarily technical in character. This in itself is a crucially important point: it means that we can have no assurance that the demand for goods and services will expand as rapidly as our capacity to produce them.

Let us assume, for example, that consumers continue to buy the same proportion of our total production in 1970 as they bought on the average during the years 1960 to 1965, namely, 65 percent of the total. On the basis of projections by such reputable organizations as the National Industrial

Conference Board or the National Planning Association,[3] this implies a rise in consumer demand at an annual rate of better than 4.5 percent during the latter half of the 1960s, or, more precisely, that consumer spending will increase by more than $100 billion over five years.

This suggests a voracious appetite on the part of American families. To achieve this increase in consumer spending, per capita expenditures would have to rise more—and perhaps substantially more—than three percent a year. This is in contrast to an average annual increase in per capita consumer spending of 1.5 percent over the long period 1929 to 1965 and of 1.7 percent during the more recent period from 1955 to 1965. It is comparable only to the urgent recovery in demand from the trough of the depression in 1933 or to the tumultuous surge in spending that came after World War II—brief periods when per capita consumer spending was rising at about double normal rates.* Note that I am not excluding an increase in total consumer outlays or in spending figured on a per capita basis: I am casting doubt only on the expectation (or, more accurately, the necessity) that consumer spending in the years ahead will sweep upward as rapidly as it did from the trough of the depression or

---

* All of these calculations of consumer expenditures are in terms of dollars of constant purchasing power, in order to measure the *real* change in consumer demand and to eliminate the distortions caused by price increases.

the immediate postwar years. Furthermore, since consumers compose overwhelmingly the largest part of the market for our production, even small differences in the rate of increase in consumer spending can have a determining influence on the overall tempo of business activity.

Yet, a prediction of the trend of business expenditures for plant, equipment, and inventory is even more complex and even more uncertain. What we are dealing with here is no ice-cold set of mechanical relationships, as we frequently see them presented, but rather with a fragile and volatile variable. From 1955 to 1960, gross private domestic investment actually declined and only in 1962 was the 1955 level surpassed. We surely could and probably will have such stagnant periods again. They are typical of the history of free enterprise economies that run to excesses of optimism and give us little or no basis for projecting any particular rate of growth in these types of outlays in the future. In any case, recent authoritative studies suggest that, even under optimistic assumptions, the demand for capital goods may grow more slowly than the requirements of the economy as a whole.[4]

5.

What happens if demand and supply fail to mesh? With an unavoidably accelerated rate of growth in the number of people seeking work, thanks to the high birth rates of the postwar years, and with the technological achievements of our scientists and business leaders proceeding at a startling pace, our capacity to produce goods and services is certainly going to grow more rapidly in the next ten years than it grew even during the prosperous ten years just past. But we have no equivalent assurance that our willingness and ability to buy will grow at the same rate.

The arithmetic of pessimism is just as disturbing as the arithmetic of optimism is exhilarating. Thus, for example, *even if* the demand for goods and services rises as rapidly as it did during the decade 1947 to 1957, but assuming also that output per man-hour continues to improve at the rapid pace of recent years, nearly ten percent of the labor force would be unemployed in 1970 and twenty percent would be unemployed by 1980. If American economic growth reverts to the long-term annual rate of three percent (as compared with nearly four percent from 1947 to 1957), unemployment could hit one out of every eight workers as soon as 1970 and about one out of every four by 1980.*

In short, unless the demand for goods and services expands as rapidly as it did in the great postwar and Korean surge of 1947 to 1957, we shall have a serious unemployment problem even if the improvements in labor productivity slow down. Or, to put it another way, if technology and automation continue at their current rate or better, we shall

---

* The calculations underlying these estimates are set forth in the statistical appendix.

have a serious unemployment problem unless the demand for goods and services grows substantially faster than it grew during the 1947 to 1957 decade; maintenance of the extraordinary 1960 to 1965 growth rates would be barely adequate to prevent a dangerous level of unemployment in the years to come.

Indeed, the problem may be even more serious than it has been painted here. All of the assumptions underlying these calculations are reasonable and within the limits of recent experience. There has been no distortion to produce a dramatic result. We have avoided throwing into the projections the impact of a major depression, brought on perhaps by balance of payments or credit and financial maladjustments, in which demand not only fails to grow but actually collapses. Nor have we considered the possibility that employers might resist any shortening in the workweek or that political resistances might curtail the role of government and require even greater rates of growth in expenditures by consumers and business firms. Yet each of these excluded factors would make the problem substantially worse than it appears to be already.

6.

There is no denying the unpleasant implications. But we have strayed into error once again: the technique we have used is still only economic arithmetic, not economic analysis. Each component of the picture has been estimated separately, yet each influences the others and is influenced by them. Productivity changes, the size of the labor force, the expectations of businessmen and consumers, government policies—none of these is a completely independent variable that we can project in isolation.

One point, however, does seem clear: unless demand rises at least as rapidly as it rose during the first half of the 1960s, or, in other words, unless the expansion in demand can be sustained well above the long-term record of the American economy, we are headed for trouble. Even under the best of circumstances, the adjustment from an economy characterized by labor shortage to one with a surplus of labor can hardly be smooth and easy.

Remember that we have no guarantee at all that consumers and businessmen will increase their expenditures at a rate fast enough to provide jobs for all those who seek them. If the demands of the private sector fall short, then only the government is left to take up the slack, whether it be large or small. We have no other alternative to the waste and social turmoil of massive unemployment. Yet current attitudes toward government spending and toward the financing of government expenditures are ambivalent, confused, distorted, and biased. The persistence of these attitudes into the 1970s can be positively dangerous. The following chapters, therefore, are an attempt to take a fresh look at this subject by cutting away the myth and analyzing the reality.

Chapter 2

THE BURDEN OF GOVERNMENT*

Let us all be happy and live within our means, even if we have to borrow the money to do it with.

—ARTEMUS WARD

1.

The issue of government spending is overlaid with emotionalism, prejudice, and half-truths—on all sides of the argument. Even the very phrase "government spending" stimulates thoughts of waste, profligacy, graft, and socialism. I should like to use a more neutral expression in this

---

* For the statistical analysis and for much of the argument in this chapter and the chapters that follow it, I am indebted to Francis Bator's important and useful book, *The Question of Government Spending,* Harper & Bros. (New York: 1960).

discussion, in order to avoid carrying the extra freight that inevitably goes along with the words "government spending," but such a procedure would be cumbersome. The reader should, however, beware of the reflex actions that these words stir up.

Oddly enough, John Maynard Keynes himself viewed government spending with distaste and only as a lesser evil than unemployment. Most of his followers have shared this viewpoint. Thus, this great economist, who convinced President Roosevelt in 1934 that a government deficit was both respectable and necessary when people were unemployed, was still talking in terms of what is now generally called "compensatory" government spending—outlays to be undertaken *only* in the absence of adequate demand in the private sector of the economy and to be cut back as soon as private demands begin to pick up.

The pieces are not easily sorted out, as one aspect of the question is likely to influence and be influenced by each of the others—thus some backtracking will be inevitable in the course of the discussion. The major questions with which we must deal are these:

1. What is the significance of government spending in the light of the foregoing analysis?
2. Is the burden of government already so excessive that an increase from current levels would be intolerable?
3. What is the impact of our tax structure on economic incentives and economic growth?

4. To what use would we put a significant rise in the share of gross national product taken by government?

5. What of the arguments that government spending is too wasteful, inflationary, and generalized in its influence to be effective in promoting economic growth?

2.

In defining the burden of government spending, we must make an important differentiation at the outset.

Government spending, whether federal, state, or local, falls into two major categories: purchases of goods and services on the one hand and transfer payments on the other. The first group—outlays for goods and services—constitute a claim on the output of the economy, on the labor and resources that produce it. As these expenditures absorb a portion of the economy's total output for the use of government, they are a proper part of the analysis of gross national product with which our discussion has been concerned.

But the other government payments, such as interest on the debt, social security, and unemployment insurance benefits, involve no purchases of goods and services. Money is simply taken from one taxpayer and paid over to another. Transfer payments therefore leave undiminished the supply of goods and services available for the use of the private sector of the economy. While these payments, in other words, unquestionably involve a burden on the people who pay taxes, this is offset by the receipts of those who benefit by them: there is no net burden on the community as a whole. This is in contrast to the former case where the government goes into the marketplace and buys, say, paper clips and road-building machinery or employs workers to clip papers together or to build roads: then labor and resources are absorbed by the government and consequently are unavailable to the rest of the economy.

Of course, transfer payments are important. For one thing, the taxpayer has little interest in whether his taxes are financing transfer payments or purchases of goods and services—it hurts him just as much either way. Furthermore, transfer payments can influence the level of demand if, for example, the proceeds of taxes on high incomes are redistributed among the poor—this may be beneficial since the poor spend a larger proportion of their incomes than the rich. But the opposite could happen, too: the tax burden on those who have to carry it may reduce economic incentives and curtail investment expenditures.

The point is that the impact of transfer payments on the trend of business activity is primarily a question of tax *structure* and is therefore not a net cost in the sense that we are seeking to define it. We will turn to the tax problem later. At this point we are really only concerned with the relationship of government purchases of goods and services to the level of gross national product. Admittedly, the pattern of transfer payments is important and can have a significant influence on business activity. But in measuring the burden of government, we can ignore transfer payments and work solely on the volume of expenditures for goods and services.

3.

In absolute terms and without adjustment for the rise in the price level, the upward sweep in total government[*] purchases of goods and services seems staggering. The figure passed through the $100 billion level in 1961, which was 20 percent higher than in the relatively recent year 1957, more than double the 1950 level, seven times as high as in 1940, and nearly twelve times the figure for 1929. State and local outlays have risen nearly tenfold since 1929, but federal spending has multiplied more than sixty times in the same span of time. One hundred billion dollars is a large number even in our economy, but it is truly enormous in terms of business activity in other countries: it is more than enough to buy up the 1960 exports of all the countries of the world, excluding the United States—all the oil, all the wheat, all the iron ore, automobiles, machine tools, textiles, and so on. And at this writing, total government purchases of goods and services exceed $130 billion a year.

---

[*] The expression "total government" refers to federal plus state and local activities.

The Burden of Government

But a good deal of the increase in government spending over the past 30-odd years was simply the result of a rise in the price level. Just like all the rest of us, the government has to spend almost $3.00 today to buy the same quantity of goods and services that could be bought with $1.00 in 1929. Thus, in real terms, the quantity of goods and services going to government today is about five times the 1929 level, not twelve times, as the crude dollar figures seem to imply.

This still exaggerates the real increase in government spending. With the growth in population over the years, we should expect government spending to have risen in any case—more people means more need for schools, roads, policemen, street lamps, post offices, and tax collectors. It also means that there are more of us to share the expenditures for defense, foreign aid, and domestic law and order. Therefore, if the rise in government spending is adjusted for both the increase in the price level and the growth in population, the resulting figure—the real volume of government purchases per capita—has only just about tripled since 1929, doubled since 1940, and, in fact, rose only 20 percent from 1952 to 1965.

But we are still overstating the increase in the impact of government on the economy. Not only are there more people in the country, but the total output of goods and services has expanded tremendously. The more we produce, the smaller burden a given quantity of government spending will be. For example, the government currently absorbs about 20 percent of our total output, but this same level of government spending would be a heavier burden if our output were smaller than it is. Indeed, the present ratio of government spending to GNP is little higher than the average of about 15 percent that prevailed during the 1930s and the late 1940s; since 1953, the total output of the economy has risen as fast as government spending, so that *the 20 percent ratio has held constant for more than ten years.*

The trends in government spending are also worth analyzing with the defense effort subtracted out. Most people are agreed that the magnitude of the defense effort is going to be determined primarily by what happens in the rest of the world rather than by what happens in the United States alone—our nondefense outlays are, however, more controllable internally and therefore a major concern in this discussion.

If we deduct national security purchases, the so-called burden of government spending is neither large as an absolute magnitude nor is it significantly greater than it was in the "good old days" before the New Deal came to power. Measured in dollars of constant purchasing power—that is, after adjusting for changes in the price level—total government nondefense outlays have only slightly more than doubled since 1929, and the rise since the end of the Korean War has been negligible. On a per capita basis the figure for the first half of the 1960s was no higher than it was in 1939. As a matter of fact, in 1929 total nondefense outlays were 7.5 percent of nondefense GNP (i.e., GNP less national security expenditures) and about 12 percent from 1960 to 1965: in other words, the "burden" on the civilian economy increased modestly. The recent level of this ratio has actually been no higher than the figures that prevailed during the years immediately preceding World War II.

Nor is this money being exactly frittered away on boondoggling. About one third of it goes for our public education.* Transportation—the highway program, maintenance of city streets, airport and water port construction— takes about one-fifth. Two-fifths of it is spent on public health and sanitation, police, fire protection, prisons, and natural resources. The small remaining balance covers what we spend for public utilities, general administrative expenses, housing, community redevelopment, veterans, and agriculture.

Of course, it would be a gross distortion to say that we are neglecting the public sector or that people would never agree to support additional efforts in this direction. A great deal is being done, and there is widening recognition of the need for ever larger expenditures of this type. Where the difficulty lies is in the uneasy feeling haunting most people that the current trend is somehow dangerous and unsound.

---

* The reader should remember that all these data, unless otherwise specified, include state and local as well as federal expenditures and taxes.

However, let us note that the ratio of nondefense government spending to nondefense GNP is smaller in the United States than it is in more welfare-conscious countries like England and Sweden, but it is impressive that our ratio is also lower than in strongly capitalist and conservative countries like West Germany and Belgium.[1] This suggests that we can go further in strengthening and improving our schools, roads, public health, and preservation of law and order without fearing that we will somehow destroy the character of our society.

But the case can be made even more strongly: we have no evidence to suggest that government spending for goods and services, even including defense spending, has starved the civilian area of the economy or stunted the growth of consumption and capital formation. As a matter of fact, as we have already noted, the postwar era witnessed an unusually high rate of expansion in these components of gross national product. Our major concern is that they were moving ahead at a probably unsustainable rate.

Important as it is, the flourishing civilian economy is not the only evidence that government was a "burden" that was easily supported. To make the case that we have had an excessive level of government spending, evidence would have to be laid out to show that we are suffering from an excess of schools, that our civil servants are overpaid relative to their counterparts in private industry, that our urban centers are models of order, cleanliness, and clear traffic flow, and, indeed, that we have more than enough soldiers, sailors, missiles, submarines, and bombs to defend the United States. I am unaware of any evidence that would support such a conclusion.

We can sum up at this point, then, by stressing that the burden of government spending in recent years has been an amazingly light one to carry. The additional amount that each household has had to finance has been small; relative to total income and the economy's total production, the rise has been negligible; the empirical evidence argues that the private economy has been a burden to our public sector, rather than vice versa.

4.

If the weight of the evidence points to the conclusion that the government has absorbed a relatively small and painless proportion of the country's productive capacity, this is still an inadequate measure of the burden it may impose on the economy. We must now ask whether government spending, regardless of size, is likely to retard or advance our economic progress. Does a shift of resources from private to public use drain the civilian economy to the point where we might actually grow more slowly with the additional government spending than we would grow without it?

There is a long and respectable tradition for an affirmative response to this question. George Humphrey, President Eisenhower's influential Secretary of the Treasury and a distinguished business leader, put it succinctly in the following colloquy before a congressional committee:

Question: Then you don't believe in compensatory government spending?

Humphrey: No, I don't think so, Joe. I don't think you can spend yourself rich.[2]

The basis of this position really is that the American people know how to spend their money "better" by themselves than their public servants can spend it for them. President Eisenhower himself summed it up this way:

> When it comes to the advancing and expanding of our economy, that is by and large the business of Americans; the federal government can help, but . . . our federal money will never be spent so intelligently and in so useful a fashion for the economy as will be expenditures that would be made by the private citizen, the taxpayer, if he hadn't so much of it funneled off into the federal government.[3]

The ultimate conclusion of this argument, of course, is that "the least government is the best government." But then it is vulnerable—and extremely vulnerable at that—to the attack of *reductio ad absurdum*. What would be the consequences of a major shrinkage in government activity? Would economic growth be accelerated by sharp curtailment or elimination of police protection, street lighting, public schools, law courts, care of the mentally ill, administration of the antitrust acts, unemployment insurance benefits, road and urban traffic improvement, public parks, communications satellites, cancer research, sewage disposal, and weather service? If, as these programs were cut back, our taxes were cut at the same time, would we spend the additional take-home pay available to us in such a way that the economy would progress faster than it did before the cuts in public programs were initiated?

Professor Galbraith has made an apt riposte:

> Alcohol, comic books, and mouth wash all bask under the superior judgment of the market. Schools, judges, and municipal swimming pools lie under the evil reputation of bad kings! ... *The difficulty with this argument is that it leaves the community with no way of preferring the school. ...*[4]

Galbraith's choice of the phrase, "the evil reputation of bad kings," catches the gist of much of the resistance to government spending. This resistance is rooted in the tradition of history, when what the government spent was actually for the enrichment or enjoyment of the rulers rather than for the improvement of the community. One need only think of Rameses the Great, Nero, Charles V, Henry VIII, Louis XIV, and Nicholas II to understand the meaning of this. The arrogation of labor and resources by the monarchs was for the purpose of building their tombs, providing them with luxurious living on unparalleled scales, or defeating other ambitious monarchs who blocked their path to power. The community as a whole was at least provided with employment that might otherwise have been missing, but, at the same time, the activities of the monarch provided little or no enrichment for the general population and frequently resulted in widespread impoverishment.

But democratic governments play a fundamentally different role. The enlargement of government activities may provide a job for a new civil servant, or open up additional business for some private enterprise, but the objective of these activities is to improve the community, not to enrich the President or the Governor or the Mayor. We build public schools, not pyramids; hospitals, not palaces of Versailles. We prepare for the common defense against an alien way of life, not for the establishment of our ruler's right to the succession of a foreign crown. We collect taxes to finance the uplifting of the general welfare, not to swell the bank accounts of the tax collectors.

This basic difference between the role of government expenditures under autocratic and under democratic government was handsomely stated by Professor James Tobin of Yale as follows:

> Classical economic ideology invests the processes by which private firms and households decide how much and on what to spend with rationality, sanctity, and purity. In contrast, the decision mechanisms of politics and bureaucracy are regarded

as haphazard and often sordid. This contrast can be maintained only by an unduly cynical view of democratic political processes and an excessively idealized picture of the decision processes of consumers and businessmen.[5]

The choice, in short, is not between public spending and private spending. Rather it is between things that advance our welfare and prosperity and things that we can readily do without, whether in the public or the private domain.

5.

However, within the context of the basic problem with which this book is concerned, the choice is actually an even simpler one. It is only at the full throttle of maximum employment that we must choose between wasteful and useful activities, between the proverbial guns and butter. As long as we have unemployed resources, we can enjoy both frivolity and high purpose (from whichever source) at the same time.[*] Of course, all other things being equal, high purpose is to be preferred to frivolity, but *faut de mieux* the most important consideration is that

---

[*] The private sector has no monopoly on frivolity nor has the public sector sole responsibility for providing us with the finer things of life.

people must be able to earn a living and support their families. In an unforgettable and famous passage, John Maynard Keynes made this point twenty years ago:

> When involuntary unemployment exists . . . "wasteful" . . . expenditure may nevertheless enrich the community on balance. Pyramid-building, earthquakes, even wars may serve to increase wealth, if the education of our statesmen on the principles of the classical economics stands in the way of anything better . . . The Middle Ages built cathedrals and sang dirges. Two pyramids, two masses for the dead, are twice as good as one.[6]

The problem, in other words, ceases to be whether we can *afford* a higher level of government spending. Rather, it is transformed into the question of whether we can afford *not* to have a higher level of government spending. Webster defines "afford" as "to incur, stand, or bear without serious detriment," which poses the issue for us perfectly. Can the United States, with its economic system at bay throughout the world, incur, stand, or bear without serious detriment the heavy load of unemployment that our earlier calculations showed as likely in the course of the coming years? When the problem is approached in these terms, *the choice will no longer be between more government and less government—it will be between more government and more unemployment.*

The Burden of Government

Government spending must be seen as part of the dynamic process of economic growth. To see it in a static setting, in which every enlargement of government outlays is sure to squeeze the private sector of the economy, is to blot out the very essence of economic development. Only with an understanding and appreciation of the dynamics involved can we avoid having the argument dominated by the twin bugaboos of inflation or crushing tax burdens.

In the static case—that is, where the volume of production in the economy is constant—it is obvious that any increase in the share of output going to the government sector must take goods and services away from the private sector. The opposite, of course, is also true: any increase in the flow of goods and services to consumers and businessmen will necessitate a curtailment in the amount available for community projects. All of this is valid and pertinent when the economy is operating at maximum capacity and full employment: when, in other words, output can be increased only slowly and painfully over an extended period of time.

This position loses all sense, however, in the case where the volume of aggregate production is rising, and especially where unemployed labor and resources exist to accelerate that increase in output. If we talk about a piece of cake of a given size, for example, then obviously some of us must do with less if others get larger pieces to eat. But when we can bake a bigger cake, at least one of us and possibly all of us can have a larger piece. As a matter of fact, our entire discussion up to this point has been centered on the possibility that we may be able to bake a cake so big that none of us will have a great enough appetite to eat it all.

In other words, a higher level of government spending will be no "burden" to the private economy if the labor and resources available to supply both sectors are increasing. Thus, for example, if our total productive capacity actually does expand to about $860 billion in 1970,* compared with $542 billion in 1960, and if we devoted *half* of that increase to the expansion of the public sector of the economy, the private sector would still increase by nearly 40 percent or from $440 billion to $600 billion. Is this too little? On the contrary, the percentage increase would actually be as great as the growth achieved during the highly prosperous postwar decade of 1947 to 1957. It would therefore seem rather difficult to argue that an expansion of 160 percent (from $100 billion to $260 billion) in the public sector would be a "burden."

This is just an example of what we can accomplish with a vigorous and growing economy. It is, however, still a form of economic arithmetic—the emphasis on the dynamics cannot be disregarded.

If the demands of consumers and businessmen grow too slowly, output may fail to reach $860 billion without a substantial rise in government spending. To put the matter

---

* See Statistical Appendix; all figures are in dollars of 1965 purchasing power.

very simply indeed, the private sector may stand a better chance of increasing by 40 percent if government purchases of goods and services expand by 160 percent than if the growth in government spending is held to some smaller amount.

6.

As shocking as this statement may seem outside the context of these pages, the burden of government is a minor consideration. In terms of the size of the American economy—in dollars and in people—it is smaller than in many other capitalistic countries and has shown no marked tendency to rise in recent years. Our civilian economy has flourished, but pitiful pockets of poverty are apparent in the public sector. We must recognize that most government spending goes into projects that help advance the general welfare. Not only will future growth in the economy help us to carry an expansion in projects of this type, but expansion of the public sector may well provide the necessary stimulus to growth in the private sector.

But before we examine some of the possible projects to which we might direct our attention, an important question remains: Where will all the money come from? We turn now to the unpleasant subject—taxation.

Chapter 3

THE FEAR
OF TAXES

Neither in Great Britain nor in the United States is there any convincing evidence that current high levels of taxation are seriously interfering with work incentives. There are, in fact . . . a number of good reasons for believing that considerably higher taxes could be sustained without injury to worker motivation should the need arise.

—G. F. BREAK

The Effects of Taxation on Work Incentives

1.

Nobody likes to pay taxes. In a way, this is curious, because most of us want, many of us enjoy, and few of us would discard the things that our tax dollars buy. We take pride, and sometimes more pleasure than we should, in being a mighty military nation. We want schools, roads, police protection, public parks, and hospitals. Indeed, we are persistent and vocal in our complaints if these services are not provided to our complete satisfaction. Meanwhile, most of us do everything we can to pay as little tax as possible (including a large amount of ingeniously rationalized cheating)—and even then, the grumbling about the government's immoral taxing powers is a national pastime.

The reasons for this schizophrenic attitude about the public purse are readily apparent. Generally speaking, we have little or no choice about paying taxes, while we at least have an option to say no to any expenditure for a private purpose. Then, after the taxes have been paid, we have no direct say in where and how the money will be spent: we can choose freely between a mammoth automobile and a sports car for ourselves, but we have little influence on the community's choice between a new fire engine or a bus—or not buying either. Finally, most of the things we buy with our after-tax dollars are for our own use and enjoyment; most of the things our tax dollars buy we use or enjoy only as a member of the community, in the company of thousands or millions of fellow citizens (many of whom we would just as happily have nothing to do with).

Therefore, even though our tax money does go to provide things that we need and want, the business of minimizing taxes has become as vital an economic incentive as the classical economic motive of maximizing profit:

each of us tries to shift as much of the tax burden as possible to the other fellow. We might be embarrassed to ask our neighbor to share the cost of our new automobile or washing machine, but we apparently have little hesitation in trying to increase his share of the cost of the local garbage collector's salary.

As a matter of fact, the resistance to paying higher taxes is so strong and automatic that we seldom stop to think objectively about what is really involved. A simple illustration will suffice. If I buy more food for the family to eat—say, an extra quart of ice cream or a larger turkey at Thanksgiving—I pay out more money at the supermarket, but it does not occur to me that my *cost* of living has risen: I have voluntarily increased my family's *standard* of living. Yet if my taxes go up in order to pay for better roads or more police protection, I grumble about the rising cost of government and the crushing burden of taxation, without taking into consideration that my public standard of living has also been improved. I will allow the butcher and the candy store to sell me more, but I will deny the politicians the opportunity to improve the quality or size of public services.[1]

Despite these attitudes, the lesson of history is that taxes can be raised and then raised again without calamitous effects on the structure of society. An interesting explanation of how this contradiction can persist has been suggested by two English students of public finance, Alan T. Peacock and Jack Wiseman. In normal and relatively settled times, resistance to higher taxes is stubborn and strong. Thus, whatever the current burden of taxation might be, it sets an effective upper limit to the rate of growth in public spending. But in times of crisis, people accept tax burdens and also methods of raising revenue that would be considered intolerable under more normal conditions. When the disturbance is over, however, the tax burden is seldom allowed to ease off to its previous levels:

> It is harder to get the saddle on the donkey than it is to keep it there ... Thus, periods of disturbance are likely to be periods in which it becomes possible to close the "gap" between ideas about tax burdens and ideas about public spending, and to do so by an upward shift in the volume of both taxation and expenditures.[2]

There is little doubt that we shall all be paying substantially larger taxes in 1970 than we were paying in 1960 whether we like it or not. This will happen in any case as our incomes rise in step with economic growth. It may happen through changes in the tax structure. It may, in fact, develop through an increase in tax rates. But the important aspect of the matter is that the growth in government revenues is not necessarily the same thing as an increase in the tax burden we shall have to carry. In 1965, our take-home pay was $465 billion out of total personal incomes of $531 billion; if, by

1970, personal incomes have risen to, say, $600 billion,* the government could take as much as $185 billion away from us in personal income taxes—a rise in the effective income tax rate from 12 percent to about 28 percent—and still leave us the same disposable income that we had in 1960.

Of course, the odds are very small that our tax payments would increase threefold in ten years. Yet it is important to realize that the community can carry a higher level of government activities as long as our incomes are growing. And, let us remember, our incomes may fail to grow as rapidly as they might *unless* we have an increase in government spending.

2.

Our tax bite is nevertheless likely to increase even if tax rates are left just as they are. This is the natural result of a progressive income tax structure in which each increment of income is taxed at a higher rate than the previous one. We pay 17 percent federal tax on the first $1000 of taxable income, for example, but we pay 19 percent on the next $1000, and these rates step up to as high as 77 percent on all taxable income in excess of $200,000.

---

* This would be consistent with a 1970 GNP of $815 billion, 50 percent above 1960.

Furthermore, as our communities are improved and extended, property values improve and property taxes therefore go up, too.

Recent studies indicate that the prevailing tax rates work out so that each rise of 1 percent in national income should be associated with a rise of at least 1.4 percent in income and property taxes. Corporate income taxes move roughly in step with national income, while excise taxes lag slightly behind (probably because we spend a larger share of income on services as we grow more affluent). Overall, we should expect a rise of 1 percent in gross national product to be associated with an increase of at least 1.2 percent in total government receipts.[3]

For example, in 1960 total government receipts on GNP account—that is, excluding transfer payments as described in Chapter 2—just about covered the $103 billion that government bodies spent on goods and services. This accounted for 19 percent of the 1960 GNP of $542 billion. Now, if GNP in 1970 rises to $815 billion, for a climb of 50 percent, we should expect total government receipts to increase by at least 60 percent (i.e., 1.2 times 50 percent) to a minimum of $165 billion, or 20.2 percent of GNP.

One thing this bit of arithmetic reveals is that our tax structure is considerably less progressive than we might like to think it is. If in theory we can afford to turn over to the government a larger proportion of our incomes as we become wealthier, an increase in our taxes from

19 percent to 20.2 percent of GNP seems like a relatively light touch compared with a 50 percent growth in our incomes. With a GNP of $815 billion in 1970, average family personal incomes would be in the area of $10,000 of 1965 purchasing power, which would leave plenty of room for a heavier tax burden than we now carry.

But even if the theoretical procedure were acceptable—that is, even if we accept as adequate a rise of 1.2 percent in government receipts with each 1 percent increase in GNP, there is reason to doubt whether it will work out in practice. Our tax structure seems to have sprung some mysterious leaks. For example, the relationship between personal income taxes and pretax personal incomes has hovered between 11.5 and 12 percent ever since the tax reform of 1954, despite a rise of 80 percent in personal incomes from 1954 to 1965.

Large amounts of high incomes must be escaping the steep tax rates to which they are theoretically subject. This is achieved through devices such as tax-exempt bonds, family trusts, stock options, expense accounts, and use of the personal interest deduction, and, in addition to such perfectly legitimate arrangements, other less savory techniques are also being employed to an increasing extent.

And then there is the conversion of regular income into capital gains, where the effective tax rate is at least half and frequently less than half the regular rate. According to Treasury data, capital gains account for only 1½ to 2 percent of total incomes below $15,000, but this percentage rises to almost 42 percent in the million dollars and over class.[4]

Many people have the impression that the tax rates on upper incomes are so high that the spread between large and small incomes has been significantly diminished. The steep tax rates are supposed to skim off a large proportion of upper incomes. After all, the married couple with a taxable income of $4000 will pay only 15.5 percent or $620 in federal income tax, while the married couple with a taxable income of $20,000 will pay $4380 or 21.9 percent in taxes, and a couple with a taxable income of $52,000 will pay $19,260 or 38.4 percent in income taxes. But it is amazing to note that in 1962 the top 20 percent of the income receivers took in 45.5 percent of total personal incomes before taxes and that they still had 43.8 percent of total personal incomes after taxes: the share of this highest group was hardly cut down at all as a result of the higher tax rates to which they were theoretically subject. The top 40 percent of the income receivers took in 68.2 percent of total personal incomes before taxes and still had 66.9 percent of total personal incomes after taxes.[5] Thus, because of the isolation of substantial amounts of high incomes from the tax bite, it is hardly an efficient machine for equalization of incomes.

The picture emerges even more strongly in a final statistical maneuver, In 1962, families with gross incomes of $12,000 paid an average income tax of $1140, or 9.5 percent of their incomes. This means that they actually paid tax on about $5500. In other words, their deductions, exemptions, and tax-exempt income amounted to the substantial sum of $6500, or more than half of their gross incomes. Families whose gross incomes averaged $34,600 paid an average income tax of $4332 or 17.6 percent of their incomes. They were paying on taxable incomes of $17,000, indicating that over $6000 of deductions, exemptions, and tax-exempt income was involved.[6]*

These data show that large amounts of high incomes escape the income tax net and accrue to their owners on a tax-free basis. This is frequently used as an argument to reduce the rates on high incomes, since they bring so little revenue in the first place. For example, the Committee for Economic Development, an effective and broad-minded group of businessmen, has argued that:

> ... very little of the total yield of the individual income tax comes from the rates above the minimum rate of 20 percent in the first bracket ... The rates in excess of 20 percent account for less than one-seventh of the total yield of the individual income tax ... The tax rates in excess of

---

* These data are confirmed by Harry C. Kahn, *Personal Deductions in the Federal Income Tax,* Princeton University Press for the National Bureau of Economic Research (Princeton: 1960), He shows that the tax yield in 1953 was hardly more than three-quarters of what it would have been with the same rate structure and no deductions (Table 6, p. 29).

50 percent produce only 2 percent of total individual income tax revenues. But they do great damage to the rest of the tax system and to the economy. Only advocates of the most extreme wealth and income redistribution deny that rates reaching as high as 91 percent on personal incomes are harmful.[7]*

But how can they be harmful when such a large proportion of high incomes is never actually subject to them? And what is the point in reducing rates on areas of the income span that now escape taxation in the first place? If the man with a $12,000 income pays tax only on $5500, can he possibly care whether the rates on the next $6500 of income are lowered? Even if the rates on this increment were cut in half, he will attempt to avoid them just as long as they remain above zero.

On the contrary, we can see how unprogressive our tax structure really is and what a small share of rising incomes is likely to find its way into the coffers of the federal treasury. This is more than a matter of social justice or advocacy of "extreme wealth and income redistribution." One's position on the matter of progressive tax rates is really dependent, not on social questions, but on the assumptions of economic analysis on which a view of the future is constructed.

---

* The 1964 tax bill reduced the top bracket from 91 percent to 70 percent as well as reducing the first bracket rates.

45

Note how crucial the assumptions are. If one believes that individuals and businessmen will have virtually insatiable demands as incomes rise, and if one assumes further that expenditures by the private sector are "better" for the economy than government expenditures, then the larger the size of after-tax incomes, the greater the stimulus the economy will receive. But if one accepts instead the distinct possibilities that the demands of consumers and businessmen will fail to keep pace with the accelerating increase in the labor force and the improvement in output per man-hour and that the public sector can also bring economic benefits—then economic growth becomes strategically dependent upon higher levels of government spending.

The analysis can now be carried one step further and related back to the tax structure. Under the first set of assumptions—vigorous private demands and value scales that prefer private to public spending—any increase in taxes would hobble the private sector by taking away money that consumers and businessmen would have spent on goods and services. But in the second case—private demands still growing, but too slowly—the increase in tax revenues to finance the higher level of government spending would be drawn from incomes that would not have been fully spent in the first place (or else the assumptions lose their validity). In these terms, it is essential that a progressive tax structure recapture a proper share of the increase in income generated by rising levels of government expenditure.

3.

Of course, while many people have come around to the idea that higher levels of government *spending* may promote economic growth, they are certainly reluctant to accept the proposition that higher levels of *taxation* can have any result except to stifle growth. It is generally believed that the best way to stimulate progress is to cut taxes, not increase them.

I do not take issue with this highly respectable and hallowed concept, but rather with the assumptions that are implicit in it. If the assumptions are valid, then of course the conclusion must follow. But I doubt whether the assumptions can hold up.

First of all, this position assumes that lower taxes would unleash a great wave of spending by consumers and businessmen. But for economic growth to be accelerated, the increased spending by the private sector must be *greater* than the volume of government spending that would have to be cut out because of the reduction in tax revenues.* If the rise in private spending is smaller than

---

* Of course, if tax revenues were reduced and government spending maintained, there would unquestionably be a net increase in the demand for goods and services. There is a practical limit, however, at least of political dimensions, to the government deficit that would be tolerated. Then we would be back to the question of whether the rise in private spending would be as great or greater than the reduction in government spending.

the cut in government outlays, income and employment would decline. If the rise in private spending is equal to the cut in government outlays, there is simply a shift in the flow of output away from the public sector and toward the private sector. For the tax reduction to promote economic growth, consumers and businessmen must spend *all of their tax savings and more besides.*

Certainly no one actually knows what would happen if we cut taxes as incomes rise. But the effect would have to be highly favorable in order to provide us with full employment during the coming years when the labor force will be increasing so rapidly.

For example, let us suppose that gross national product does rise from \$676 billion in 1965 to \$1350 billion in 1980.* Let us also assume that we decide to reduce taxes as our incomes rise, so that the share of gross national product that government can purchase will tend to decline (although it may rise in absolute figures). If government's share is cut from its current level of around 20 percent to a lower figure of 15 percent in 1980, government purchases of goods and services in 1980 would be about \$200 billion, compared with \$122 billion in 1965. By the same token, however, if the total demand for goods and services is to reach \$1350 billion, purchases by consumers and businessmen would have to rise from \$554 billion in 1965 to \$1150 billion in 1970—an increase of 100 percent or 4.8 percent a year.

---

* See Statistical Appendix.

But such a rate of growth in demand would be most unlikely without some currently unexpected stimulus appearing upon the scene. Private demands will have to be exceptionally strong, but the pressure for higher living standards among consumers or for radical technological change among businessmen shows no evidence of being that intense.

Where the desire for a better way of life is strongest—that is, where the largest proportion of an increase in income is likely to be spent for goods and services—namely, among the lowest-income groups, the effect of tax reductions would be virtually meaningless. Families with incomes below $4000 pay less than 5 percent of their gross incomes in federal income taxes; state income taxes are negligible; the burden of excise taxes must also be minimal as most of their expenditures are devoted to necessities. As their total federal income tax payments amount to only about $2 billion, complete elimination of their income taxes would hardly start a major prosperity on its way.[8]

There is of course the possibility that a reduction of corporate income tax rates might be stimulating, if the cut in taxes were passed on in lower prices. This would be particularly the case on goods of a luxury or semiluxury nature or where foreign competition has been eating into domestic markets.[*]

---

[*] In technical terms, price cuts will be salutary where demand is elastic.

This position misses an important objection. Is there any reason to believe that corporations would reduce their prices if their tax burden were lightened? On the contrary, prices went up in 1945 and 1946 despite a sharp cut in corporate income taxes; the same thing happened after 1953 when the Korean War excess profits tax was taken off. On the other hand, no marked change in the price trend occurred after the tax cuts of 1964 to 1965. The point is that businessmen charge—quite rightly—precisely what the market will bear. Prices are reduced only if goods are not selling at current price levels. If people continue to be willing to pay $5.00 for shirts and $3000 for cars, changes in corporate income taxes will be irrelevant to the price-setting decisions of businessmen.*

Perhaps the strongest—or, at any rate, the most trumpeted—argument in favor of tax reductions is that they would enhance incentives, while rising taxes are supposed to blunt incentives.

---

* It is worth noting that the opposite is also the case. Costs do not "push" prices up. If customers refuse to pay higher prices, businessmen will hold the line even if their costs do increase (either that, or go out of business). In the short run, rising costs are an excuse for rather than a cause of rising prices. In the longer run, higher costs affect prices only through eliminating marginal producers and thereby reducing the supply of goods offered for sale (or reducing competition for the stronger producer).

Yet, although no one actually enjoys paying taxes, the history of the postwar period provides little evidence that economic incentives have been sapped. Even though tax rates were much higher than they had been in the prewar days, and especially in the pre–New Deal days, economic growth since 1947 has not only been more rapid than it was during the 1920s, it has clearly been more stable. Gross private domestic investment in particular has maintained an historically high average level despite frequent predictions of its demise. A traveler passing through the United States could not help being struck by the fantastic number of shining new factories, office buildings, and homes in every city he visited. The flow of new ideas, new products, and new technologies since World War II is as great as in any period of our history.

Of course, the argument has been made that these investments were made in the expectation of earning large profits. The greater the expectation of profit, this theory runs, the greater the investment that will be undertaken. Therefore, a reduction in taxes that increases net incomes will lead to an expansion in investment. The final proof offered for this position is that, without exception, the years of high profit since World War II have been years of high investment, while investment has declined in the years that profits have shrunk.

But like most correlations, this fails to tell us which is cause and which is effect. Investment is the dynamic force in a free private enterprise economy: consumer spending seldom varies except in response to changes in personal incomes. Assuming government spending unchanged, then, incomes, output, and employment will rise only if investment rises first. And investment is keyed to future, not current, levels of demand. In short, when businessmen are optimistic and bold, investment expands and draws the rest of the economy along with it—including profits. We can see accordingly that the chances are as good that the high investment *causes* high profits as that high profits cause the investments to be made.

Furthermore, despite the grumbling, can we find any reliable sign that individuals are using high taxes as an excuse for laziness?

Corporate executives in the highest tax brackets seem to be working as many Saturdays, Sundays, and evenings as ever. Columns like "Personal Business" in *Business Week* magazine, that discuss the living habits of these executives, give the distinct impression that they work too hard and play too little. The stomach ulcer and the premature heart attack have apparently not been made obsolete by high taxes that persuade people to take life easy.

Indeed, the main complaint about inadequate incentive (or, to put it less graciously, a strong distaste for hard work) has been directed toward the wage and salary workers with incomes at $7500 a year and less. Widespread annoyance has developed, especially toward service workers, now that the "working class," liberated from the hot breath of poverty and the nightmare of unemployment, is less inclined to jump at the master's whip. But to the extent that this is true (or undesirable), it would be difficult to pin the blame on the tax structure, for it was higher real incomes and employment security, not heavy taxes, that have made for less frenzied work habits.

Indeed, do rising wages draw more people into the job market and inspire them to work harder? Or do rising wages make it possible for the main breadwinner in the family to provide adequate support so that his wife can stay home to take up golf and his son can go to college? Do low wages make people work harder so that they will earn more, or do low wages give people a strong distaste for work because they get so little from it?

We do not know the answers to these questions. However, the relation to the tax-and-incentive argument is plain. Higher taxes reduce take-home pay. A progressive tax structure makes each increment of net income increasingly difficult to achieve. If people want to get ahead in the world—and the presumption is that lower-income workers have more incentive to move up the line than have upper-income employees—there is at least as good a chance that high taxes will make people work harder as that they will lead people to exhibit a notably larger degree of laziness. It is the schoolteacher and the fireman who engage in moonlighting, not the vice president of the billion-dollar corporation, which thus suggests that people with small incomes still have the desire—or need—for larger ones.

In this connection, a foreign comparison is relevant. In the postwar era, West Germany has been held up as a model of free enterprise, as an outstanding example of the application of conservative fiscal and monetary policies, and as an unquestioned leader down the pathways to economic growth. Yet West Germans pay more of their gross national product to the government in the form of direct and indirect taxes than we do. In addition to West Germany, the tax load in Austria, Finland, Norway, France, Sweden, Luxemburg, Britain, the Netherlands, and Italy is higher than in the United States (and in that order).[9] It is worth noting that all of these countries showed a faster rate of growth during the 1950s than we did.

One explanation, perhaps, is that high taxes may actually stimulate economic activity by making the government a partner in losses and expenses as well as in profits and income. Risk-taking is encouraged as a result. The United States government in effect subsidizes 50 cents out of every dollar that business firms spend on the research and development from which so much of our growth is supposed to come. The risk of taking on additional employees, extra overhead, more services, and expanded advertising has been reduced because a substantial part of the money paid out for these purposes would have gone to the government in taxes in any case. An entire new world of luxury eating and entertainment has emerged from government-subsidized expense accounts that have given many corporate employees an opulent way of life they never could or would have paid for out of their own earnings. These facts give us good reason to ask whether a lower level of tax rates would really increase risk-taking proclivities. Or would it instead induce a wave of penny-pinching and cost-cutting that would in fact intensify the problem of achieving full employment in the years to come?

In short, we have little or no evidence that our present tax structure is an impediment to economic growth. But that is more of a negative than a positive case for higher levels of government spending. The issue turns as well on the alternative uses of public as contrasted with private spending.

Chapter 4

THE USES OF GOVERNMENT

*We have always known that needless self-interest was bad
morals; we now know that it is bad economics.*
—FRANKLIN D. ROOSEVELT
January 20, 1937

1.

The case against asking all of us to pay more money to
the government in taxes rests on three grounds: (1) that
it restricts our freedom of choice in spending our money
in accordance with our individual wants; (2) that it retards
economic growth by stifling economic incentives; and,
finally, (3) that it destroys growth by shifting productive
resources from private to public use.

The nub of this position, the essential assumption upon which it depends, is the third one: the things that people buy for themselves are inherently superior for the public welfare than the things that the government provides for them. Much of the necessity for arguing about incentives and economic freedom would melt away if the opponents of high taxes could establish beyond question the superiority of private over public wants.

Here is how the Committee for Economic Development (CED) states the issue:

> We do not accept the view that as our economy grows federal expenditures should necessarily grow in proportion, or more than in proportion to the increase of national income. On the contrary, if we behave wisely, it should be possible for federal expenditures to decline relative to national income as per capita incomes rise—aside from the unpredictable requirements of defense. With higher incomes, people should be better able to provide for themselves some of the things for which they now look to government. The level of generally available services that government should provide would require a smaller proportion of national income.[1]

But there are two highly debatable assumptions implicit in this argument. The first is that, in the absence of a higher level of government spending, there will be an adequate level of private spending to provide full employment—note the automatic assumption on the part of the CED that private spending will provide a sufficient impulse to keep national income expanding at a desirable rate. We have already analyzed this question in considerable detail. The second assumption is that "people should be better able to provide for themselves some of the things for which they now look to government." Although we have touched on this, we must now examine the proposition more thoroughly.

2.

In the first place, we must recognize that the pricing mechanisms of government services and of the products of the private economy are fundamentally different.

Privately produced goods and services are priced to cover their entire cost of production and to show a profit, of course. But more is involved than that. The full cost, including profit, is paid by the user of the product. I pay no part of my neighbor's automobile, nor does he contribute to the cost of my dishwasher.

In the public sector, on the other hand, the process is entirely different. Certain services—toll roads, the post office, public power, and the dog licensing department, for example, are paid for largely (not necessarily completely) by those who use them and are, indeed, sold at a "price." But the rest of the public services, and this includes by far the largest share, have no "price." Each taxpayer pays in accordance with how much wealth and income he has and *without regard to the degree to which he avails himself of the service*. My taxes pay for the schoolteacher's salary and the park department's trucks, whether or not I have children and whether or not I ever set foot in the park.

The reasons for this are clear enough but of primary importance. If I want a new automobile or a suit of clothes or a trip to Europe, that is my own business and payment for it is equally all my own responsibility. But schools, parks, police protection, sewage disposal, and national defense are essential services for the community that make life better for me whether I use them directly or not. The schools will determine the quality of our democracy and our labor force; the parks clear the streets of cavorting children; the police department prevents and detects crime and keeps traffic moving and organized; sewage disposal prevents disease; national defense protects our physical property and our way of life.

The entire community would suffer if any of these public services were removed or eliminated, while only a very few people would be involved if I failed to buy a new car or a new suit or a trip to Europe. Indeed, these public services are so essential to all of us that the direct use each of us makes of them can hardly be the determining consideration in how we pay for them. My own sewage may be very small and my neighbor with a big family may create a great deal, but I may get cholera if his sewage is not disposed of—should I be relieved of contributing to the cost of this service?

Since the benefits of these public services are thus virtually impossible to determine in the case of each individual citizen and since the community as a whole would be unable to operate properly without them, payment can hardly be based on the direct use that each person may make of them. If the poorer citizens were required to pay their per capita share, their private living standards would be seriously depressed; in terms of equity, they would be paying more than their share, for the wealthier persons could more easily afford to make the same dollar payment. Therefore, the concept of ability to pay was made the cornerstone of the tax structure; the wealthy, who have the larger amount of money to spend after paying for the private necessities of life, must carry a proportionately larger burden of the cost of necessary public services than the poor, who spend most of their income on private necessities already.

This justifies the maintenance of some public services that operate at a clear loss instead of a profit, because they are profitable to the community as a whole. We all benefit from the existence of a postal system. In fact, our economy could not function without it. Even though I never write or receive a letter, my entire way of life depends upon the existence of a postal system without which the people I employ, from whom I buy, and to whom I sell would be unable to communicate cheaply over any distance at all. Postal service is as essential as sewage disposal. Why then must it operate at a profit? Why shouldn't it be subsidized by the community and by those who make little direct use of it, since the entire structure of the community would collapse without it?

The subsidization of commuter railroads can be justified by many of the same arguments; which is why increasing numbers of them are moving and will continue to move into public ownership. For example, I am a confirmed city dweller and fail to understand the attractions of suburban living for many of my friends. If they want to go through the agonies of commuting back and forth from work, I would be tempted to say that it is all their worry: why should I subsidize the New Haven Railroad so that it will cost my friends less to get in and out of town? The answer is that having them out of the city solves many problems: the city needs fewer schools, fewer police, fewer water mains. Furthermore, if the commuters go in and out by train, the traffic situation in the city is significantly relieved. In these terms, it would be unfair to ask them to pay the entire cost of the railroad service, since I receive benefits from it as well.

Subsidized public housing is another interesting but probably more controversial example. Without it, the people in the lowest-income groups would continue to live in slums: their incomes are too small to carry the full cost of decent housing facilities (or at least, too small to carry them without drastic cuts in other aspects of their living standards). But their incomes are also too small for them to be able to afford trips to Europe and fur coats; no one is suggesting that the community should subsidize those things for them, so why should the community subsidize their homes? The answer is that the community will get along all right if some people are unable to see Paris or to wear mink, but slums are a blight to the city, a source of crime, ugliness, filth, and disease. Everyone's way of life is lowered and threatened by slums. Thus, the guiding principle is still valid: the service is so essential to the entire community that we must all contribute toward its cost. We would be wrong to ask only those who make direct use of it to carry the full burden.*

Therefore, the CED makes a meaningless proposal in suggesting that, "with higher incomes, the people should be better able to provide for themselves some of the things for which they now look to government." Let us assume for the sake of argument that the postal system, the pursuits in cancer research, low-cost housing, commuter railroads, and even electric power in the Tennessee Valley

---

* In a curious way, we all subsidize one another through what the economists call "consumer surplus." For example, because of the economies of large-scale production, 6 million automobiles can be produced and sold more cheaply than 3 million cars. But this means that the second 3 million buyers have in effect subsidized the first 3 million, for the first 3 million would have to pay substantially more for their cars if the demand were limited to 3 million instead of expanding to 6 million.

could all be provided more efficiently by private industry. Nevertheless, the issue is not how efficiently the service is provided, but whether only those who make direct use of it should bear the entire cost involved. If substantial benefit inures to the rest of the community, then the service belongs within the public domain, with its cost shared by all members of the community.

The position of the dividing line defined by this principle is the point at which the political Right is separated from the political Left. There is no dispute that the national defense, preservation of law and order, and sewage disposal belong in the public domain. But when we come to housing, medical care for the aged, electric power, and public transportation, the controversy becomes considerably hotter. The difference of opinion goes deeper than the necessity for such projects to operate at a profit to the government—the real question is whether these enterprises belong under communal arrangements in the first place. The full socialist, of course, would argue that all production is so imbued with community interest that everything must be included in public ownership, while the old-fashioned conservative would cut the public sector to the barest minimum. The experiences of the depression and the war, however, have convinced the great majority of American citizens that communal interests go further than we were once willing to admit. In the words of the great economic historian, R. H. Tawney:

It is not till it is discovered that high individual incomes will not purchase the mass of mankind immunity from cholera, typhus, and ignorance, still less secure them the positive advantages of educational opportunity and economic security, that slowly and reluctantly, amid prophecies of moral degeneration and economic disaster, society begins to make collective provision for needs which no ordinary individual, even if he works overtime all his life, can provide himself.[2]

3.

Essentially, then, the uses of government spending are profitable to the community. This is something quite different from saying that they would be profitable if they had to pay for themselves as going businesses. Rather, the point is that the community is better off with these things than it would be without them.

But there is another crucial assumption inherent in the statement that the provision of public goods and services is profitable to the community: we must also establish the contention that the private goods given up in exchange for the public goods (to the extent that a choice must be made) would provide less satisfaction and welfare than the public goods that took their place. Profitability, after all, depends upon the rewards exceeding the costs.

The Uses of Government

There is a general bias in the public mind, and a fully articulated position held by the political right, that the things people buy for themselves are by their very nature superior to what they receive from government. It follows that government spending must therefore be a drain on the community and, furthermore, that a reduction in taxes and public spending will naturally lead to a rise in living standards. Seen from this position, the uses of government can never be profitable to the community. In fact, at its extremes, this point of view seems to imply that *all* taxation is a loss to the community, because no government expenditures can bring any benefit. For example, here is a statement by a leading business executive, Robert C. Tyson, chairman of the Finance Committee of United States Steel:

> Since an accountant must ever balance the books, I point out that whatever good is done by the spending must be balanced against the evil done by the taxing. Taking value from Peter to pay Paul does not increase total value one iota; instead the value is undoubtedly in some part dissipated, if only by the overhead costs incurred in its transfer. Since a Cassandra would indulge in prophecy, I suggest that this nation will encounter disaster if it continues to ride the fantastically rising curve of total taxing and spending it now bestrides.[3]

Considered further, the illogic of this position may become clear.

Although we are hardly the fully rational Benthamite version of the economic man, on whom classical economics was constructed, we are still a long way from being irrational beings. We do order some priority to the goods and services we demand—that is, we choose bread before caviar, blankets before slip covers, permanent dwellings before summer cottages. We buy the most essential things first and then add on the less essential, the luxuries, and the frivolities afterward.

Now, therefore, the assumption is undoubtedly correct that we are providing ourselves with all the necessities we can afford and that, as our incomes have risen, we have subsequently built up varying layers of more luxurious and less essential goods and services. But it follows from this that a reduction in taxes would have little effect upon our consumption of the highest priority goods and services, which are already provided for: we would instead add on another layer of less essential goods and services. This is especially the case in the light of the tax structure. Certainly, the upper-income groups are already comfortably taken care of in meeting the necessities, while the lower-income groups pay so little in taxes in any case that a tax reduction would give them only a very small additional sum of purchasing power.

But in the public sector we are still sorely lacking high priority, necessitous goods and services. If we accept the premise that our welfare would be improved by more education, better roads, urban renewal, less juvenile delinquency, better-balanced defense programs, less poverty in foreign lands, and so on and on and on, then the choice between expansion of the public versus the private sector takes on a different guise. We shall have to do without private goods and services of relatively low priority, but we shall receive in exchange goods and services that the community generally agrees are highly desirable—if not, in fact, essential—for our economic well-being.

This is not to deny that *some* privately consumed goods and services may have a superior priority to the services of the public sector: we need basic rations of food, clothing, and shelter before we can start worrying about education, roads, the Bureau of Labor Statistics, and even the provision for common defense. However, in the American economy most of these basic private needs are reasonably well met and those who lack them would receive little or no benefit from a tax reduction, while major public needs are as yet unfulfilled. Therefore, the substitution of additional nonessential private goods for more essential public ones through a reduction in taxes and government spending would actually *lower* our living standards, not raise them. It is true that we might feel momentarily richer. But in the long run, the choice of fewer public goods will cost us dearly.

This analysis suggests that we have no assurance that the decisions of consumers in a market supplied by profit-oriented producers will necessarily be more efficient in catering to their wants and needs than the choices they make communally through the payment of taxes and the spending decisions of their elected representatives. Where the lure of profits and the market economy supply the needs of the community, no issue exists—the system will tend to provide the largest quantity at the lowest cost. But where there are needs that a profit-oriented economy will fail to meet, this is no reason to argue that such needs have a second-class character whose satisfaction can readily be postponed.

4.

Let us take education as an example. What priority shall we choose to attach to more and better education? Do we want this more or less than the goods and services that we might buy ourselves if our taxes were reduced? During the 1960s, the number of children from kindergarten to eighth grade will rise 30 percent, while the numbers in the ninth to twelfth grades will rise 50 percent. Is adequate provision for this expansion worth more than the crimp that paying for it may put in our private living standards?

Of course, it is true that the schools earn no profit. That probably explains why our per capita expenditures for liquor and tobacco are double the amount we spend for education or why we spend more than half again as much on amusements and entertainment as we spend for education.

As another example, how would we compare the advantages of higher private living standards with the need to solve the complexities of increasing urban concentration?

From 1920 to 1950, our citified population increased from 51 percent to a little over 60 percent of the total population. It is now more than 70 percent and still rising. These trends present staggering problems, for urban communities require much more in the way of public facilities than rural areas.

Professor Philip M. Hauser, chairman of the Department of Sociology of the University of Chicago, has estimated that an investment of $1000 per capita is needed for urban services and that, as a result, "$33 billion must be invested during the 1960s alone merely to provide such services for the anticipated *increase* in the metropolitan area population."[4] To this figure must be added the investment cost of bringing existing facilities up to an adequate level of performance, for no one could argue that our public services function with an optimum degree of efficiency.[*]

Mr. Reginald Isaacs, chairman of the Department of City and Regional Planning at Harvard University, has some additional somber comments to make on this subject:

---

[*] An even more staggering figure of $65 billion *a year* has been cited by the National Planning Association (*Looking Ahead,* Vol. 9, No. 4, May 1961) to cover a program of "modest" improvements in urban renewal and development.

It is obvious that we are thirty years behind time in the use of metropolitan planning techniques ... Given limited population and metropolitan sprawl, new definitions and practices of freedom and government will have to be devised. These will not be achieved merely by multiplying those we have now ... Drastic urban renewal to meet even modest standard levels will require a quadrupling of present-day expenditures, perhaps even a quarter of our gross national revenue. Both revolutionary planning and drastic renewal call for rational behavior of a kind presently unacceptable to a people whose goals are in terms of personal reward and almost unlimited freedom to meet those goals ... Were Boston to spend a billion dollars toward solving its traffic problems by 1970, it would then have reduced the problem only to the level of what it is today.[5]

Or, to shift the scene—but not to desert the main line of the drama—let us consider the question of foreign aid. If there is a great need for funds to relieve domestic urban strangulation, the requirements for capital in the underdeveloped areas of the world dwarf our own.

Little elaboration is needed to emphasize the pitiful standard of living in which the great mass of the world's population is forced to live. The concept of a saturated market is certainly unique to the small number of countries that we can call developed. While per capita gross national product in the United States is $2800 and while the top 29 percent of the world's population (including the United States) has a GNP for each person of a little more than $1100, the remaining vast majority of the world's people produce only slightly over $100 each—and of that $100, an even smaller sum is available for their own consumption and enjoyment. Indeed, the top 8 percent of the world's population produces about 30 percent of the world's total gross national product; the lowest 50 percent of the population produces less than 20 percent of the total output.[6]

The case for assistance to the underdeveloped countries can be presented with an unfortunately lengthy list of grim, urgent facts. One will suffice here. India will require the investment of a billion dollars a year to provide housing in the urban areas just for the increase in population that will have to be taken care of over the next 25 years. This allows nothing for rural housing, for any improvement in the shocking slums in cities such as Calcutta, or for the roads, sewage systems, water supplies, hospitals, or educational facilities required for a growing population. A billion dollars a year would require as large a proportion devoted to housing from India's gross national product as we now devote to our own total residential construction activities (including repairs and replacements), but the Indian economy can far less afford this allocation of resources. Finally, the $20 billion that the Indians will have to spend for this one purpose between now and the mid-1980s is about three times the total sum lent by the World Bank since it started business, and it is equal to around five times as much as our current level of total foreign aid payments.[7]

The layers of luxury piled on top of our own standard of living are much thicker than we ordinarily realize. As one scholar recently described it:

> If we strip away from the average American family all vacation travel; television set, radio, telephone, and newspaper; almost all movies and books; all but the most elementary part of its education; all of its frozen foods, almost all canned foods, and almost all foods transported more than a few miles except salt, flour, and similar staples; all clothing but one very simple dress or suit and one pair of shoes or sandals; and, finally, say four-fifths or more of its house and all but a few pieces of furniture—if we strip away all of these, we have probably reduced the income by eleven-twelfths, but have left the family with all of the true necessities of life, and it becomes easier to understand how the lowest-income 50 percent of the world's people can live.[8]

This comment might be footnoted with the following quotation from *Life* magazine, describing a seventeen-year-old girl in Van Nuys, Cal., who is, if not typical, not extraordinary either:

The Uses of Government

> In the previous year, Suzie had received $1500 worth of clothes and $550 worth of entertainment and $102 worth of beauty parlor treatments. She owned seven bathing suits and had her own telephone.[9]

But a motive for a vastly expanded foreign aid program rests on a broader base than the obvious political and humane considerations, overwhelming as these may be.* Foreign aid can in effect be a powerful instrument to accelerate our own rate of economic growth.

In the first place, an expanded foreign aid program has uniquely attractive features as a vehicle for larger government expenditures. As a simple buyer of goods and services, the government is least likely to interfere with or to disrupt the normal operation of the economy. Even when the government pursues other programs that are relatively innocuous with respect to free private enterprise—such as building roads, schools, and hospitals—it still impinges on the private sector to some extent. Larger programs—power and resource development, housing, and aid to distressed

---

* In relation to the snail's pace at which living standards can rise in the underdeveloped lands and the incredibly wide gap between the way we live and most other people in the world live, it is amazing that we can feel satisfied with less than 1 percent of our gross national product devoted to foreign aid. It is equally little wonder that our foreign aid program earns us such little friendship and enthusiasm in the underdeveloped areas of the world.

areas, for example—are charged with explosive problems and touch areas where many businessmen are extremely sensitive about "government interference."

Foreign aid, on the other hand, involves a minimum of such interference. The government simply becomes a larger customer of American business firms. In many instances, in fact, our own government is not even the customer—the customer is the foreign government or foreign enterprise to which funds have been transferred by the United States Treasury.

Furthermore, the foreign aid program will in time make a significant positive contribution to our economic growth and our balance of payments by increasing the capacity of the underdeveloped countries to buy American exports. In the short run, of course, foreign aid helps our exports by making dollars available to these countries that they could not have spent otherwise. But there is a more profound and lasting increase in dollar earning power that will accrue to these countries as their own export capacity is increased. The capacity to export in a general sense, and, furthermore, the special capacity to export goods with a high percentage of value added and a high degree of price stability depends ultimately upon a country's per capita income, basic productive capabilities, and degree of specialization. These can be immeasurably enhanced by the capital and know-how that an effective foreign aid program can provide. It is no coincidence that our best customers are the highly industrialized countries that are already wealthy, not the underdeveloped countries that lack so much:

Destination	Total Imports of U.S. Merchandise 1965 ($ Billions)	Imports of U.S. Merchandise per Capita 1965 ($)
Europe	8.0	20.00
Japan	2.0	20.40
Rest of the world*	11.1	3.40
Total	21.1	6.40

*Excluding Canada.

While the foreign aid program will therefore probably result in an expansion in our export trade as incomes and productivity rise abroad, some people are concerned that the short run effect will be to strain our balance of payments by throwing too many dollars into the international exchanges. This is, however, a greatly exaggerated danger. In short, at least 80 cents out of every dollar we give away to underdeveloped countries comes right back to us in the form of expenditures on American goods and services—goods and services that might well have remained unsold (or sold at lower prices) if we had no foreign aid program.

Furthermore, the question of priorities is applicable here as well. In the fight against communism, in the battle for the uplifting of the human spirit, and as an investment in our future customers, the foreign aid program ranks as high as any other aspect of public policy—in some instances, it may rank higher than the defense establishment itself. Therefore, if this program should create difficulties for our balance of payments, the solution is not to be found in reducing the volume of foreign aid. Rather, other and less important payments to foreigners could be curtailed, such as American tourism or American investment in dollar-rich countries: unavoidable curtailments in the debit side of our balance of payments should be based on some order of priority. Foreign aid is among the least expendable.

5.

Government expenditure brings strong positive advantages to the well-being and economic development of the community. In the affluent society, in fact, an additional measure of government spending can bring us more benefit than an equivalent sum spent by us as individuals in the satisfaction of our personal wants—this is what Professor J. K. Galbraith describes as the Theory of Social Balance. There is a choice here, and a choice worth considering more thoughtfully than the popular clichés tend to pose it.

Mr. Robert E. Lusk, the president of Benton & Bowles, one of our leading advertising agencies, sets the issue in these terms:

Does advertising make people buy what they do not need? I do not think so. What are needs? Those of the people of India are certainly not the same as those of America, nor are our needs of today identical with those of the 1920s. We really do not need airplanes or autos or vacuum cleaners or TV sets or makeup or hair shampoo or frozen foods or even soap. But is it wrong for people to want these things, once they have been created, if people can afford to buy them? I doubt it.[10]

Of course there is nothing wrong in wanting things that we do not need. *But there is something wrong in maintaining that we can afford things (or in devoting efforts to persuading people we can afford things) we do not need when there are so many other things that we truly do need.* If the choice were between persuading people to spend money on hair shampoo and frozen foods or on nothing, I would enthusiastically opt for the shampoo and the frozen foods. This is *not* the choice, however. There are alternative uses for our labor and resources that can bring us higher as well as more wholesome standards of living. Mr. Lusk sniffs something wrong, but a nose too close to the grindstone can develop insensitive nostrils: is Madison Avenue justified in pressing the sale of goods and services we "really do not need" when the engines of mass communication spend little or no effort in convincing us of the necessity for schools, urban renewal, and foreign aid?

Chapter 5

THE TRAGEDY OF ERRORS

He who believes he can escape his destiny is only attached to a longer rope . . . But at the end of the rope . . . we shall have to do quite freely that which it was necessary for us to have done in the first place.

—JACQUES DEVAL

1.

The opposition to higher levels of government spending is thickly encrusted with worn slogans, half-truths, and angry arguments. We have already dealt with some of them, and shall treat three others here. But we must not lose sight of the essential point: the statistical analysis in earlier chapters indicated that the labor force is likely to increase faster than the level of employment in the years ahead, unless the expenditures for goods and services by governmental agencies is accelerated to supplement the demands of the private sector.

This shifts the focus of attention to where it should be. The objections to increased government spending are valid in varying degrees. But the objections to *lower* levels of government spending are even more overwhelming, because the alternative may be massive unemployment and a mushrooming of our already excessive burden of community poverty. Therefore, the harshest, the most dogmatic critics of government spending must not be permitted to cripple the public budget; rather, we must take note of their arguments to improve our public policies and to make government spending more effective in its impact upon the economy.

For example, we frequently hear that government spending is wasteful, it is inflationary, and its effects are too broadside and generalized.

There may be an element of truth to each of these accusations. This means that if government spending is wasteful, we must devise methods to squeeze the waste out. If it is inflationary, we had better seek policies to keep the price level stable. If it is inadequate to deal with localized problems, we shall still need an expansionary environment within which those localized problems will become soluble. Even though government spending may create difficulties, in other words, the need for higher levels of public expenditure will exist.

As we shall see shortly, the error in each of these criticisms is not that they are irrelevant to the consideration of government spending *but that they apply with equal importance to the private sector of the economy as well.* This is the crucial point that reveals the true character of the objections these critics raise. Since their complaints about waste, inflation, and shot-gun policies are only partially valid and apply to the private sector simultaneously, they are merely a smoke screen to hide a more fundamental objection—to the shift of resources from private to community use. This is where we shall ultimately find the real area of controversy.

2.

The previous chapter dealt in part with the question of the wastefulness of government spending. We attempted to answer such questions as these: Do the outlays of public bodies contribute less to the welfare of the community than the outlays they replace in the private sector? If we reduce taxes and encourage an increase in consumer spending and private capital formation, would the additional private goods meet our needs more fully than the public projects that we would have to abandon?

In the light of this examination and set in the environment of the prospering nation, public expenditure appears to be wasteful to only a minimal or marginal extent. Most of it makes a positive contribution to the welfare of the community. What really bothers us is not that government spending is wasteful—but rather that *there is waste in government spending.* This is something entirely different. It accepts the ends of government spending but limits the quarrel to the means. It recognizes the futility of throwing out the baby with the bath water.

By the same token, it is relevant to draw attention to the waste that exists in the private economy: the production of low priority goods and services is by no means the monopoly of public servants. That this waste creates employment when it occurs under the aegis of the National Association of Manufacturers is grounds for dignifying it with the title of planned obsolescence; when it occurs in government, we complain about boondoggling.

But we can find waste in the process of private production itself as well as in the goods and services that the process yields. A top federal civil servant is paid less than $30,000; the salary of high-level people in most state and local government is far less. But in private industry, especially in the big companies that account for the largest proportion of our production, a salary of $30,000 is for the middle-rank executive, on the threshold of Bigger Things. If we believe that $30,000 is the most that we are willing to pay the men we retain to carry responsibility and make decisions that affect the life and welfare of all of us, is it economical to pay many times that sum to the Madison Avenue scribe, the genius of the soap business, or the steel company executive who loses his company's market to competitive materials and nations?

Of course, businessmen are not the only architects of private waste. Their employees have a substantial vested interest in it as well. Whether the dispute is centered on work rules or just plain featherbedding (or coffee breaks), many industries are groaning under the weight of a heavy layer of overemployment, which the unions are fighting a bitter rear-guard battle to defend. Can anyone who has ever watched deny that we are building houses or providing rail transportation today without a painful burden of waste?

The prevalence of waste in the private sector is of course no excuse for ignoring it in government. Rather, the point is that Americans are accustomed to waste at all levels and that powerful vested interests have been built up to preserve it. The danger in overemphasizing its importance in government is the threat that this implies to the very existence of activities that are far from wasteful for the community. In short, we must distinguish between the false notion that government spending is wasteful and must therefore be curtailed and, on the other hand, the true but far less sweeping suggestion that government functions might be handled with a greater degree of efficiency.

3.

As planned obsolescence in private production is renamed boondoggling when government spending is involved, so have the opponents of government damned an increase in government spending as inflationary while hailing expansion in the private sector as economic growth and dynamic prosperity. Because this nomenclature has some historical veracity, the stereotypes it creates tend to linger on in the public mind. Yet government spending can make a significant contribution to prosperity and economic growth, while rising expenditures in the private sector can make a corresponding contribution to the outbreak of inflation.

Indeed, the whole dispute over the inflationary impact of government spending is an interesting example of the curiously subjective and emotional response that the concept of government spending tends to create in the public mind. Yet a dollar earned by a civil servant, a soldier, or a steamfitter working on the new town hall gives each of them as much purchasing power and as much pleasure as a dollar earned by a bank clerk, a Pinkerton detective, or the welder working on the new office building. But the same opponents of government spending will argue simultaneously that, rather than being less "potent" in its effect on the economy, a dollar's worth of government outlays on goods and services will have an intensely inflationary impact compared with what happens when private individuals or businessmen spend an equivalent amount of money.

In order to untie this knot, we must define precisely what we are talking about. This is more important than one might think. Everyone has become an expert on inflation. The humblest housewife and the distinguished professor of economics discuss it with equal assurance and knowledgeability, along with the ditchdigger and the corporation president. Like communism and juvenile delinquency, we all fear inflation and are supposed to want to get rid of it—but can't help being fascinated by it at the same time.

We can begin by saying that inflation means a rise in the general price level—that is, an increase in the prices of most goods and services that is not offset by price declines elsewhere in the economy. It is also frequently, but not necessarily, defined as a process which tends to persist and become self-perpetuating—in other words, price increases in one area lead to price increases in others, while the rise in money incomes that accompanies this process leads in turn to further rounds of rising prices.

The causes of inflation have been much disputed in recent years. Originally everyone agreed that inflation occurred when money incomes or the money supply rose faster than the supply of goods and services available to be bought with that money. In other words, the general price level moved upward in response to an overall excess of demand over supply. But on occasion, the postwar American economy has been treated to the phenomenon of rising prices in industries where idle capacity and excessive inventories were clear signs that no shortages existed.*

---

* For example, from the 1957 peak to the 1959 trough in business activity, output of iron and steel dropped 40 percent while prices rose over 2 percent; machinery prices went up 5 percent while production fell more than 20 percent; production of motor vehicles declined 40 percent while prices were raised 4 percent.

This led to a new hypothesis that the upward pressure of costs, especially labor cost, was a potent factor in the inflationary process. Thus emerged the great debate over demand-pull versus cost-push theories of price inflation.

More sophisticated analysts have come to recognize that this is a chicken-and-egg type of problem in which cause and effect are impossible to distinguish. Rising costs and rising prices are inevitably *associated* with each other, but that is not the same thing as saying that one is caused by the other. In any case, no matter where the truth lies in this particular aspect of the controversy, we are in the happy position of being able to ignore it: it is irrelevant to the central question of the inflationary influence of government spending.

We can disregard it for two reasons.

In the first place, responsibility for cost-push inflation rests upon the combination of union monopolies and corporate positions of market power in the *private* economy. These influences persist despite and not because of the amount of spending by public bodies. To some extent they are a function of the general level of economic growth and development, but they are in no way directly linked to the volume of government spending.

Second, even in the case of cost-push inflation, demand is a critical factor. No businessman raises his price if he fears a more than corresponding drop in the quantity of his production that he can sell. That prices have risen in industries with excess capacity is no proof that the law of supply and demand has been repealed; rather, it shows that demand in these industries is relatively insensitive to price and is determined primarily by influences other than price. But this means that a true understanding of the inflationary process, even from the cost-push viewpoint, must ultimately get back to the analysis of supply and demand.

In the classic inflationary case, prices begin to rise because demand is created without a corresponding rise in supply. Specifically, workers are paid to produce for nonconsumer markets—for the government, for business capital formation, or for foreign customers outside the country. But these workers want to spend their earnings on food, clothing, shelter, etc.; they neither can nor wish to buy an army truck, a machine tool, or the goods being shipped abroad. Thus, their incomes have increased, but the supply of things available to them has failed to increase.* Demand then exceeds supply, and the inflationary spiral commences.

However, if this sequence of events is to result in inflation, certain necessary conditions must be met.

---

* In rare instances, inflation can begin as a result of a spontaneous rise in consumer spending itself. Thus, after World War II, consumer demand was financed, not by higher employment, but by drawing down liquid assets that had been accumulated during the war. The fundamental situation was the same, however: consumers wanted to buy more goods and services than they were producing.

First, there will be no inflation if idle labor and resources are available to expand the supply of consumer goods in response to the rising demand. Some brief increase in prices may occur at the beginning due to localized supply bottlenecks, but this will only be a signal to businessmen that demand is rising and that they should put idle labor and resources to work producing more of the goods whose prices are going up. In other words, inflation is unlikely to occur, or will occur only briefly, under conditions of elastic supply.

Second, even if the total physical supply is limited by full employment of labor and other productive resources, inflation may still be avoided if consumer *demand* is also held in check. This will depend upon the manner in which the additional government spending, business investment, or export shipments are financed. If the government levies heavier taxes* or if people decide to save a larger proportion of their incomes, then the failure of the supply of consumer goods to increase along with higher incomes will be matched by a restriction in consumer demand.

If the additional government spending or business investment or export shipments are financed by the creation of new money, then—assuming full employment

---

*The taxes must of course draw in money that would otherwise be spent. If the higher taxes have no effect on consumer spending decisions, then the inflationary process will continue even with a balanced government budget.

of labor and resources of course—inflation will almost
certainly occur. The additional funds paid out in wages
and salaries to the workers supplying these nonconsumer markets will leave the spending power and spending decisions of other consumers untouched. The new
money will compete with the old purchasing power in
the marketplace for consumer goods. As demand will
then be excessive under conditions of inelastic supply,
prices are sure to rise.

Since, however, supply is seldom completely inelastic, inflation of the type just described is relatively rare
under normal peacetime conditions. To the extent that
it does occur, it is usually brief and mild. For example,
during the investment boom of the mid-1950s, gross private domestic investment rose from 13.5 percent of gross
national product in 1954 to more than 16 percent in
1956; wholesale prices, which had been stable for four
years, rose 4 percent between 1956 and 1958 and then
stabilized again. Indeed, rapidly expanding demand often
makes possible the introduction of cost-saving innova-
tions by businessmen that help to keep prices stable. It is
significant that our total output increased 22 percent
from 1961 to 1965 while prices rose only 6 percent; during the preceding five years, output increased only half as
much and prices rose more than 7 percent.

Large, persistent, and cumulative inflations really occur
only under the economic impact of war, which explains
the association in the popular mind that limits the cause of

inflation to government spending. In wartime conditions, the expansion in the demand for nonconsumer goods is both rapid and substantial—from 1941 to 1944, for example, federal government purchases of goods and services swelled from 13.4 percent of the gross national product to 42.1 percent. Furthermore, the employment needs of the armament industries are added to the manpower requirements of the armed forces, thus almost certainly limiting and frequently reducing the labor force available to produce consumer goods. Despite exhortations to save and the repression of consumer demand by higher taxes, it is politically impossible to avoid recourse to the money-creating process. Wartime provides the perfect mixture of ingredients for the inflationary cocktail.

The reference to history is important. In less democratic times, monarchs and barons frequently debased the currency in order to finance fruitless wars or gigantic "wasteful" public works like Versailles. Men were drafted from their homes and from the farms: these men still wanted to eat and be clothed, while the output of food and clothing was reduced. With additional quantities of money being put into circulation to pay for the king's pet projects, a rising supply of money chased after a diminishing supply of goods. Inflation was the inevitable result.

Our historical memories therefore play tricks on us. With a reflex action, we equate government spending with inflation and, subconsciously, with the "evil reputation of bad kings." But while government spending obviously *can* cause inflation, that is not at all the same thing as the contention that it *must* cause inflation, or, in fact, that inflation is caused *only* by government spending.

The preceding should make this clear. In the first place, as long as idle resources and idle men are available, an increase in government spending will have little or no inflationary impact. The extra employment it creates will require no shift from the private to the public sector; it will draw on the unemployed. The increased demands of these newly employed people will be met by drawing still further from the ranks of the unemployed and putting them to work producing consumer goods. Indeed, much of Chapter 2 stressed that we will be able to enjoy a substantial rise in both public and private spending; with the flood of new workers coming into the market, there need be no competition between the two sectors to meet the requirements of each.

But if we do reach a point of full employment and limited supply, and inflation then does occur, this is still an inadequate basis on which to pin the blame on government spending. What about the increase in private investment or in exports that will also take place? As we have seen, inflation can come about when we employ men to build railroad cars or machine tools and pay them wages that they want to spend on food and clothing: this is just as inflationary as employing them to build roads or guided missiles under conditions of full employment and an expanding money supply.

The point is that inflation is the result of an excess of *total* demand over *total* supply. To point the finger at and assign responsibility to government spending is like indulging in an argument over whether a glass of water is half full or half empty. Are prices rising because government spending is excessive? Or because consumers want—and advertisers are urging them—to buy more goods at current prices than there are goods available for them to buy?

But the opponents of government spending are not yet ready to retire from the fray. They will admit that, under conditions of full employment, inflation can occur when investment rises and is financed by newly created money. This is precisely what happened from 1955 to 1957. But they insist that a government-induced inflation will by its very nature be more intense and protracted than an investment-induced inflation, because private investment involves expenditures on new plant equipment and inventory that will ultimately lead to an increase in the output of consumer goods.

Although this is undeniable, the word "ultimately" is strategic. The investment process can continue for a long time; indeed, the increased productive capacity that it creates may be used to turn out still more capital goods instead of consumer goods. The economic problem of the underdeveloped countries, regardless of the economic and political system that they have chosen, turns on just this point: as long as they must devote such a large proportion of their output to building capital, the supply of consumer goods will rise at a maddeningly slow pace and inflationary pressures will remain intense.

This argument also rests on the additional untenable premise that only private investment will increase the productive capacity of the nation. Yet public investment is also a potent force in economic growth. Admittedly, the defense program proper leads to little direct increase in the capacity to produce goods and services needed by the private sector, although atomic energy, a new world of electronics, and space communication are examples of significant by-products of our defense effort.[*] But a large proportion of nondefense expenditure also increases the nation's productive capabilities: roads, schools, dams, sewage disposal, public health centers, river and harbor improvements, the preservation of law and order, weather forecasting, the collation and interpretation of economic statistics, street cleaning, labor exchanges, the supply of technological information to farmers, retraining of workers, and the maintenance of public lands are just a few obvious examples.

Thus, the essential point remains intact. Inflation occurs under certain limited and unique conditions. Even

---

[*] For manufacturing as a whole, 43 percent of outlays for research and development in 1960 were for military products. See McGraw-Hill, *14th Annual Survey of Business Plans for New Plants and Equipment, 1961–64.*

if these conditions exist, they are no more "caused" by higher government spending than by higher private spending. In most circumstances, both can lead to the ultimate increase in the supply of goods and services that will snuff out the inflationary fires.

4.

But a final obstacle remains—the problem of overcoming structural as opposed to cyclical unemployment. In the former case, we refer to unemployment that is caused by special conditions in a particular industry—technological progress, loss of markets due to obsolescence, or persistent downward pressure on prices from competing materials or imports. This type of unemployment is, in theory at least, independent of the general level of business activity. It tends to be permanent, in that jobs lost as a result of these factors are likely to be eliminated forever. On the other hand, cyclical unemployment involves jobs that are lost as a result of fluctuations in the general level of business activity. Here the loss is probably temporary, in that employment opportunities will open up again when business conditions improve.

If the level of unemployment is primarily structural rather than cyclical in nature, the argument is made that government spending would be the wrong medicine to cure the illness. If labor-saving devices are destroying jobs in autos and steel, if low-cost imports are cutting into the market for textiles and watches, if aluminum and plastics are replacing steel and copper, then it will be no good, according to this position, to pay higher salaries to schoolteachers, to build new hospitals, or to give fertilizer and farm machinery to underdeveloped countries. Even worse. If the economy is generally fully employed outside of the sick industries and if the increased incomes resulting from these increased public expenditures are spent in the general economy, the impact of the government programs could be inflationary even though large numbers of men are still unemployed.

This is invalid on two counts.

First, it again makes government the sole villain of the piece, when private industry may be in the same position. For example, let us assume that all of the unemployment in the economy is structural. Then any broadside program of government spending or any public expenditure outside the depressed areas would have only a delayed and indirect effect on employment rates there and might simultaneously ignite inflationary embers in the rest of the economy. But obviously *any* increase in expenditure, *any* effort to expand output in the operating sector of the economy will have the same effect, *whether it occurs in the public or the private sector.*

Thus, if it is a mistake to raise teachers' salaries, build hospitals, and ship agricultural equipment abroad, it is equally wrong to improve the pay of stenographers, produce more television sets, and export commercial aircraft. If we oppose a rise in government spending because it will fail to cure structural unemployment, then we must oppose just as vigorously any sign of growth or expansion in the private sector (or at least we should be entitled to express some skepticism regarding its effectiveness in reducing the burden of unemployment).

Second, government spending may still be justified even if it fails to cure the ailments of structural unemployment. The reasoning is simple. The only cure for structural unemployment is retraining and relocation of the displaced workers into occupations and areas where growth is rapid and demand is expanding. Very well. But unless growth in the rest of the economy is sufficiently rapid so that jobs are opening up for these workers, then how will we know which skills we should teach them or which localities we should direct them to? The inflationary tinges that may result from a higher level of government spending would be just what the doctor ordered—signals of shortages, signals we need to guide in the placement of the displaced workers.

If the private sector of the economy is growing fast enough to absorb these surplus workers and if the rate of growth is sufficiently marked so that we know how to retrain and relocate them, then of course we have no basis for advocating higher government spending as a means of relieving unemployment. But that does not exclude us from advocating higher government spending on other grounds. It simply means that we are back to the earlier arguments in this and preceding chapters with respect to the choices between public and private expenditure. And if we shift our assumption from rapid growth in the private sector to slow growth, then the urgency for a higher level of government expenditure becomes correspondingly more intense.

It is true that the fundamental problem with which this book is concerned is much closer to the cyclical than the structural character of unemployment, for the difficulty of absorbing the young new entrants to the labor force is determined essentially by the overall rate of economic growth. But we are vastly oversimplifying if we think that a vigorous rate of growth is the full answer to the difficulties posed by structural unemployment. The strongest force in growth is technological progress, much of which tends to be labor-saving. We gain little, in other words, from an increase in productive capacity that is accompanied by a minimum increase in employment opportunities. This means that we must heed the direction and quality of economic growth as well as the crude percentage rate of increase in output. In this context, government spending again emerges as a desirable solution: the major areas of government spending are in construction and in services, both of which use relatively large quantities of labor per unit of output.

5.

No matter how we view the question, then, the choice of the optimum level of government spending is essentially one between public and private needs. This is the issue that is all too frequently obscured by disputes over the side effects. There may be waste in government spending, it may have inflationary implications, and its influence may be insufficiently specific—but the same objections may be raised against private spending. The nub of the matter is the direction that we want the economy to take. If growth in the private sector is too slow, a rise in government spending is the only alternative to a crushing and dangerous burden of unemployment. If we are at or reasonably close to full employment, then we must decide where our priorities lie and which areas of the economy require the most rapid attention.

The concern over inflation and waste is a blind alley. We do not reject a solution simply because it brings problems in its wake; in any case, no economic solution is ever innocent on this score. We must restrain inflation and eliminate waste wherever they appear, but we must also assure ourselves of a vigorous, growing, and viable prosperity. If higher government spending can provide these things, and provide them more fully than private spending, then let us restrain inflation and eliminate waste—but let us have the government spending nonetheless.

Chapter 6

THE ECONOMICS OF DEMOCRACY

If animal spirits are dimmed and spontaneous optimism falters, leaving us to depend on nothing but a mathematical expectation, enterprise will fade and die. . . .

This means, unfortunately . . . , that economic prosperity is excessively dependent on a political and social atmosphere which is congenial to the average businessman.

—JOHN MAYNARD KEYNES
The General Theory

1.

The objective of the previous chapter was to show that the opposition to government spending ultimately comes down to a value judgment that the growth of the public sector is bad. Most of the conventional arguments against government spending turn on side issues that becloud this basic distaste.

If I were to ignore the tenacity with which this opposition is held—if, indeed, I were to ignore the case that the opponents of government spending make to support their value judgment, I would be indulging in a form of arithmetic optimism of my own.

It is insufficient to maintain that the public sector needs cultivation more than the private sector needs it, nor is it enough to demonstrate that higher levels of government spending will enlarge private incomes. The most critical and yet unpredictable influence determining the level of business activity is the state of expectations—especially businessmen's expectations. *We have no guarantee that an expansion in public outlays will sustain optimistic expectations among consumers and businessmen,* particularly when such outlays are accompanied by rising tax revenues.

While we have heretofore assumed that consumption and investment would rise in response to increased government spending, this essential assumption will be incorrect if fear, uncertainty, and doubt about the future of the free enterprise system are created at the same time. We shall simply be keeping company with our old friends, the arithmetic optimists: what I have presented as a form of consistent economic analysis will turn out to be nothing more than mechanical arithmetic. The influence of government spending on the state of expectations is, therefore, crucial to the entire thesis.

One important point should be established at the outset. Nothing would more rapidly erase the smiles of business optimism than government spending badly managed and badly planned. While the need for enrichment of the public sector is great and while rising public expenditures can be a powerful stimulant to the level of output and employment under the right conditions, this certainly does not warrant just any expenditure of public money. No responsible public servant can ignore business sensitivity to profligacy.

Rational control of the public purse strings is far from simple. The separation of taxation and public spending decisions builds up resentment among taxpayers but gives spending an attractive aura of costlessness to its beneficiaries. This is particularly the case with a system such as ours, in which lower-income groups receive substantial benefits from government spending but the tax burden is carried to a greater extent by upper-income individuals and by corporations. The push and pull of these forces can dangerously disorganize the operation of our governmental bodies: on the one hand, vocal and active minorities may receive an excessive share of the public bounty to satisfy special interests at no cost to themselves, while, on the other hand, well-to-do taxpayers may fight a stubborn battle against socially desirable programs, with a consequent human cost to deserving people.[1]

But the fear of a rising government budget goes deeper than localized problems of equity, or anger at waste, or the evil reputation of bad kings, or mere discomfort with the tax burden. It is a fear of change in the essential character of our economy and that much abused phrase "the American Way of Life." It is too important to be treated with the light-hearted scorn that most liberal economists and politicians show it. The association between rising public expenditures and loss of freedom is so firmly implanted in the American mentality that no properly planned program of expanded government spending can be realized unless we face up to these fears and put them to rest. This can be done only by revealing their true nature.

2.

Western capitalism in general, and American capitalism most especially, means more than the private ownership of the means of production. It includes the exchange of goods and services for money in the marketplace, where individual citizens freely seek their own best interest. It is in the marketplace that customers' choice crosses swords with producers' output, pricing, and technological decisions, and where this give-and-take of supply and demand is designed to satisfy human wants at the lowest possible cost.

At its best, this system can work miracles of economic development and do so with a highly efficient allocation of resources. The hungry search for profits can be a magnificent stimulus to improving the lot of hungry people. At its worst, however, this system will turn out socially useless goods for those who can afford to pay, while the needs of the poor are unsatisfied; it can exploit both consumer and worker through imperfections in the operation of the market; most serious, rigidities within the system and the institution of money itself can lead to savage fluctuations between deep depression and explosive inflation.

Intervention by the government into the operation of the marketplace was therefore an inevitable development—despite the frequent predictions of disaster, dictatorship, and communism that accompanied it. Ground rules have been established to give some semblance of countervailing strength to the various parties to the bargaining process. The antitrust acts, the interstate Commerce Commission, the National Labor Relations Board, the Taft-Hartley Act, the Federal Trade Commission, and many of the agencies of the Department of Agriculture are examples of direct government intervention into the free functioning of the marketplace. Even the inspector who checks the accuracy of the local butcher's scales is a member of this team.

Although this impaired our full freedom to make private economic decisions, the objective was only to redress inequities in bargaining power: within the limits set by public regulation, the output, pricing, composition, and techniques of production of America's gross national product were still determined almost completely by free private enterprise. Prior to 1933, the government was still in the position of the drama director who tells the actors how to play their parts and expresses enthusiasm or distaste for the author's work, but who neither writes the plays nor performs them on the stage.

At the depth of the depression, however, our entire economic system—and our political freedom as well—were threatening to collapse. Increasing numbers of people therefore accepted a rise in the public budget as an essential step to hasten the process of economic recovery. Sheer human need and political necessity were soon clothed in theoretical respectability when John Maynard Keynes set out to prove that our private economy would be unable to recover by itself without a shove from some outside force.

But Keynesian economics, as pointed out earlier, still viewed an increase in government spending as a temporary palliative to overcome unemployment; it assumed that the public budget would be cut back whenever the private economy took hold and moved ahead toward full employment on its own. The desirability of government spending for its own sake was never an issue.

Therefore, in the months that followed V-J Day in 1945 there was no question in anyone's mind that the enormous wartime machinery of government spending should be dismantled as rapidly as possible, so that the largest possible share of our output would be available to the private sector. If someone had had the temerity to suggest that the federal budget should be maintained around its

1944 level of $96.5 billion (it dropped to $28.4 billion by 1947), and that the money should be shifted from war production to the construction of public housing projects, the building and staffing of schools, the creation of a road network capable of carrying the millions of automobiles beginning to pour from Detroit, and desperately needed capital for reconstruction in the war-devastated countries, the poor fellow would have been remanded immediately to the local lunatic asylum, where he could have lived happily ever after at the taxpayer's expense.

In retrospect, this economic deviate appears saner than he might have looked at the time. We *did* need schools, roads, and low-cost housing. We *did* have to provide economic assistance to our friends in foreign lands. We got many other things that we admittedly needed—automobiles, clothes, household appliances, and a residential construction program notably weighted in favor of upper-income projects. But later, at much higher prices, we still had to face the ultimate necessity of paying for schools, roads, low-cost housing, and economic assistance to our foreign friends.

3.

The taxpayer's money does buy us things that we genuinely need. Yet the distaste for government spending lingers on. It lingers on because the area for freely made individual economic decisions is believed to shrink as the government's budget swells. Here is how the reasoning runs: the higher the level of government spending, the heavier the burden of taxes; the heavier the burden of taxes, the smaller the sum the citizen can spend on his own individual choices. The more restricted the amounts that private citizens can spend on the satisfaction of their personal needs and desires, the more the businessman is curtailed in the variety of things he can produce, the markets in which he can operate, and the prices that he can charge. Instead of an economy in which the composition, volume, and prices of goods and services are determined by millions of individual decisions, the single massive decision of government sets the pace. It is from this root that the smothering vine of socialism is expected to grow.

Professor Henry Wallich, one of the most articulate and thoughtful opponents of an expansion in the public sector, has set the issue in these terms:

> The centralized economy puts a strain upon democracy and freedom; the free economy does not. . . . [Because government causes] the cumulative discouragement of private and local initiative . . . , it would have to be shown that the people could do something only very imperfectly, and the government very substantially better, before the government should step in.[2]

The most cursory reading of the history of Weimar Germany, France in the 1930s, prerevolutionary Russia, and our own country in 1932 will provide a prompt denial to Professor Wallich's belief that the free economy puts no strain on democracy and freedom. But this is no answer to his main argument that a centralized economy does lead to a loss of freedom.

4.

What can we say about the problems that the single massive decision of government creates when it steps in in place of millions of decisions of individuals to buy, sell, produce, and price as they like?

There is a basic confusion involved here. If the government were to take 30 cents or even 40 cents or 50 cents out of every dollar's worth of our production, in contrast to its present share of about 20 cents, the government would then become a larger *customer* of American business. It would not be a larger producer. This is a most significant difference: a government that buys a larger proportion of our output creates neither a planned economy nor a socialist one.

In a planned economy, the government makes all the essential decisions now made by the individual businessman. The planning agency decides what should be produced, in what quantities, at what price, and then how it should be distributed. In most cases, the planners may also determine the method of production, the relationship of labor input to capital input, and the amount to be paid to each of the factors of production. In a socialist economy, the government as owner of all the means of production is even more deeply committed to the decision-making processes of economic life.

In our economy the government comes into the marketplace like any other customer. The bargaining power of such a tremendous customer is admittedly important. But businessmen can sell or refrain from selling to the government as they wish. They will certainly refuse to sell if the government's price is unprofitable to them: no law requires them to sell below cost. Except in extreme cases, such as wartime, when we have a forced-draft economy, only the lure of price and profit are available to the government—as they are to every other customer of the businessman—to establish its claim on the output of American industry.

The distinctions here are extremely important. There is a fundamental difference between a government that is a customer and a government that is a producer (or that plans private industry's production). *In a planned or socialist society, the government determines more than its own needs for the provision of public services: it also decides what goods and services will be sold to the private sector, at what prices, and on what terms. In a free enterprise economy such as ours, the government determines only its own needs and the terms on which they are to be satisfied; the private sector, however, is left free to make its own choices and decisions as to what it will buy and sell and on what terms.*

This is surely not meant to deny the existence of governmental intervention into the private economy. Such intervention, however, takes the form of regulation of one sort or another, such as antitrust actions or the controls exercised by the Federal Reserve Board. We have even experienced regulation of wages and prices, rationing, and allocation of materials. But regulation is different from and independent of the level of government spending. Intervention of this type could continue and could even increase at times when the government's share of gross national product is reduced. On the other hand, government spending could expand without bringing in its wake any more intensive regulation of the bargaining process in the private sector.

Admittedly, the taxing and spending policies of the government may redistribute income in favor of one group of citizens at the expense of another. Yet this is still different from a net reduction in the freedom of decision-making. The people losing out on this redistribution are indeed more limited in what they can do with their incomes, but this is offset by the gain that the beneficiaries of the arrangements may receive. Nor can a community that believes in freedom absolve itself from its responsibility for certain groups, such as the veterans, the aged, and the unemployables. It would be difficult, in fact, to argue that the destitute have any real freedom at all.

We must recognize, however, that this is a valid area of controversy. As long as government services are designed to benefit the community *as a whole,* we can find little basis for believing that there is a loss of individual freedom when higher incomes are taxed more heavily than lower incomes. The rich as well as the poor can attend the public schools, use the roads, sleep more confidently because of the national defense and the police and fire departments, and move more safely through the streets because the slums have been eradicated. But when government spending and taxing policies favor one group at the *expense* of the whole community, the opponents of government spending have a strong case and should be heeded.

5.

The impact of the government upon the private decision-making process is intimately related to the questions of economic growth and full employment to which this book has been addressed.

In an economy that is unable to grow, either because it is operating at full capacity or because private industry is stagnating, any increase in the government's share of production will be at the expense of the private economy. This may still be justified if the welfare of the entire community is advanced by having more public necessities and fewer private luxuries, but it may also bring with it a loss of economic freedom. Much as the individual may enjoy or require the facilities that the government provides, his freedom of choice has still been reduced.

In a growing economy, this issue appears in a very different light. Here the public sector can expand without forcing a compression of the private one. There is room for both to increase. If our gross national product rises from $676 billion in 1965 to $860 billion in 1970, while the private sector's share goes from $554 billion to $650 billion, the private sector's share of our total output would have shrunk from 80 percent in 1965 to 75 percent in 1970—but it would still be nearly $100 billion greater than it had been ten years earlier.

This case can be put still more forcefully. The number of people seeking work is going to grow twice as fast as it grew during the postwar era. Unless productivity improvements are drastically curtailed, the chances are small that the demand for goods and services will grow fast enough to absorb all these new workers without a substantial rise in government spending. We are therefore calling the wrong tune when we contend that higher levels of government spending will repress economic freedom unless we have a vigorous rate of economic growth; unless we have the higher levels of government spending, we are likely to have an inadequate rate of economic growth. In short, by contributing to and promoting economic growth, the expansion of government spending may do more to preserve our economic freedom than to destroy it.

We must never forget that the number of unemployed is more than a statistic to be studied with academic interest or pecuniary curiosity on the financial pages of the daily press. How much freedom have the unemployed? What is the enticing range of choice available to them to pass their leisure hours? Shall it be a trip to Paris or Hong Kong? A shopping expedition for a new hat or a new bangle? Should they choose to collect their unemployment insurance in New York or St. Louis? Would United States Steel or General Motors be more attractive places to be refused employment than, say, the American Telephone and Telegraph Company or Procter and Gamble? Should the growing pools of unemployed young people read the words of Thomas Jefferson and attend a play of Shakespeare—or read Mickey Spillane and listen to the mouthings of the nearest rabble rouser? An extraordinary degree of economic freedom indeed!

Even those who do have jobs but who live at the lower levels of our society have little stake in economic freedom. The uneducated, the unskilled, and the hemmed-in racial minorities have no real freedom of choice. They do not work where they would like to work—they work where a job can be found. They do not buy everything they want, but only the subsistence level they can afford.*

---

* We could really carry this one step further. In a competitive, conformist society, the degree of economic freedom throughout the social hierarchy is probably much less than we profess or believe it to be. The patterns of living are so rigidly determined by the environment around us and by the din of advertising to which we are subjected, that our choices in the marketplace are made within extremely narrow limits. And this is also true of where we work, where we live, and how we use our leisure. If, therefore, we are taxed more heavily and the government spends our money for us, the supposed loss of economic freedom under these conditions would probably cover a degree of freedom that we never had in the first place.

111

6.

The true character of the dispute over government spending may be revealed in the answers to an intriguing question: Why does the request for additional national defense appropriations meet the most enthusiastic and patriotic reception from conservative legislators who would feel strongly unpatriotic in voting money for public programs with more peaceful objectives? The military, despite arguments, can always win friends and influence people. But why are social welfare, public education, and economic assistance to underdeveloped countries such legislative wallflowers? I do not question the necessity or the patriotism involved in voting for an increase in our military capabilities. It is fair to ask, however, why it is any less patriotic to vote for other essential programs that also advance the cause of America.

One strong reason for this difference is immediately apparent. Military spending is largely outside the sphere of civilian economic existence. While of course our soldiers, sailors, and airmen have to be fed and clothed and housed, the primary business of the military is to produce and use things that never meet the commercial test of the marketplace. Housing, electric power, schools, social insurance, and scientific research are all involved in one way or another with the private sector of the economy; roads and airports disturb the railways; public health centers compete with private medical care facilities; aid to foreign countries builds up potential competitors. Not so atomic

112

bombs, submarines, missiles, and 150-mm ammunition: they are not offered for sale to the citizenry. They are kept in the preserve of the military and, in fact, are designed to be destroyed and used up in the grim business of warfare.

But there is a more subtle and profound reason why the conservative mind accepts defense spending so readily and rejects other forms of public expenditure so vehemently. In part, national defense implies that the blame for our troubles lies outside our own country, and it thereby dilutes the urgency to find solutions here at home. But what the issue really boils down to is this: most nondefense spending is socially dynamic in purpose and impact, while defense spending is not. *The national defense epitomizes the maintenance of the status quo.*

It is interesting to note that the controversy over public spending touches very lightly, if at all, on socially innocent domestic measures that are designed to keep things as they are—the police and fire departments and sewage disposal are accepted as necessary to our existence right along with a fully manned national defense establishment. But the socially dynamic areas of public spending—schools, housing, aid to underdeveloped countries, or agricultural assistance—are where the real heart of the controversy lies.

We may infer from this that the true basis of the opposition to government spending is really something different from the concern over the preservation of personal freedoms. Rather, the concern is for the preservation of social differentials. How is our freedom and democracy "strained" if our people are better educated, better housed, provided with less expensive electric power, driven on better roads, and kept in better health? How is our freedom threatened when we assist the desperately poor people of other lands to raise their living standards? How much freedom do we lose when we enable the square pegs of our society to exist peacefully among us instead of allowing them to starve or turn to crime?

On the contrary, the great upheavals of history have all had their roots in the efforts of inflexible people to repress the forward momentum of social change. We may have learned too little from the Sermon on the Mount, but only disaster has befallen those who have blocked the meek in their long march toward inheriting the earth. The terrifying ferment in which the world finds itself at this very moment has been the inevitable consequence of an excessively passionate adherence to the social status quo.

7.

The issue of government spending and personal freedom is also related to the economic competition to which the Soviets have challenged us.

The program of the Soviet Communist Party sets lofty goals for economic progress:

> Within ten years, [output increased] by approximately 150 percent, exceeding the contemporary level of U.S. industrial output.

114

Within twenty years, [output increased] by not less than 500 percent, leaving the present overall volume of U.S. industrial output far behind.[3]

The Russians have set a herculean job of growth for themselves. They are shooting for an annual growth rate of 9.6 percent a year—double our potential—for the 1960s, followed by an annual rate of 7.2 percent in the next decade. The only decade since the Civil War in which our own output went up as much as 100 percent, or about 7 percent a year, was 1933 to 1942, when we started with a vast reservoir of unemployed labor and resources. During the latter half of the nineteenth century, when we were being converted from a largely agricultural to a primarily industrial nation, our economic development was speeded by a substantial inflow of capital from abroad; the Russians, on the other hand, hope to be capital exporters in future years. This can only mean that the production of factories, machinery, equipment, and public investment will claim a significant share of their rising output, while the needs of consumers will continue to be met in far smaller measure.

In a contest of this type, our head start is an enormous advantage. Just as an example, let us assume that the Russians would like to increase their armament effort and their foreign aid programs by the substantial figure of $100 billion from 1965 to 1975. This alone would require a 3.3 percent a year increase in their output, without allowing anything for domestic capital accumulation or the improvement of consumer living standards.

On the other hand, if the American economy grows by 3.3 percent a year during this decade, our output will have risen by $260 billion from 1965 to 1975, so that we can match their cold war effort and still have plenty left over for other purposes.

In short, victory in the cold war (or a hot war) is not really dependent upon comparative rates of economic growth. The numbers game of economic growth should really be subordinated to the manner in which our economy functions and a rational allocation of our resources. It takes brains as well as dollars to get to the moon and to solve the development problems of the Latin-American countries. If we throw away our growth on luxuries alone, we will lose even if our growth rate exceeds the Russians'; if we take full advantage of the higher base from which we start and, as we can much more easily afford to do, if we direct our growth toward the improvement of world economic conditions and the remedy of shortcomings in our own society, we cannot help winning out.

Our greatest tragedy would be a failure to use our capabilities to the fullest possible extent. Nothing would be worse for our cause in the cold war than a persistent and heavy load of unemployment in this country. Although the capitalist system has done a magnificent job of providing employment and raising living standards since 1945, we must remember that it survived the 1930s by a hair's breadth. The evil reputation of the bad economics of prewar days still smolders, especially in Europe.

It can be rekindled rapidly if another economic crisis strikes the West.

There is no reason for us to emulate the Communists in everything they do. The social balance in their economy is as lopsided as ours, but it is lopsided in the other direction. They have focused more attention on the social aspects of the public sector than we have: their emphasis on education, medical care, public parks, and low-cost housing is well known. In future years, however, the pressure will be on them to raise personal living standards, while we will have to give the public sector more attention. The more they move in emulation of us, the better for everyone. Certainly the world will be a happier place when the Russians are more interested in personal comfort than in tractors and power plants.

The preservation of our personal freedom is inseparably linked to the challenge that the Russians have thrust at us. If our growth rate is inadequate, if we are burdened with unemployment, if we fritter away our rising output, the Soviet economic system will surely triumph and perhaps its military and political systems as well. But, as I have attempted to demonstrate in these pages, the degree to which we enlarge the scope and activities of the public sector will be crucial in determining the level of employment and the quality of our economic progress in future years. This is only another way of saying that a rising volume of government spending is likely to do more to protect our personal freedoms than to destroy them.

8.

Although America has never lacked for prophets of doom, they have had a hard time of it. Our history is marked with its share of narrow escapes, but the combination of flexibility, ingenuity, and optimism in our approach to life has always saved the day for us. Because we have been pragmatists more than we have been theorists, we have avoided the rigidities of dogmatism, which has given us the ability to find new ways of solving problems. Because we are optimists, we have kept seeking a solution until we have found the best one.

My purpose in this book has been neither to predict the disastrous levels of unemployment that we might have to contend with in coming years nor to deliver a polemic in favor of higher levels of government spending. Rather, I have sought to define a problem that will grow in intensity with the passage of time, and to suggest the possibilities of a solution that can be most attractive if we will face it with honesty and enthusiasm.

We are always warned about the costs of too much government spending, but we are seldom told of the costs of too little: the gist of my thesis has been that these latter costs may become heavy ones indeed. The accelerated growth in our labor force is not a problem that will solve itself without any action on our part, but a higher level of government spending will not be a satisfactory solution *unless we can cut away the thick crust of dogma that surrounds it.*

The Economics of Democracy

All the economic analysis in which I have indulged will be meaningless if we fail to approach this problem with our traditional flexibility and ingenuity. Even with an increase in government spending, full employment cannot be achieved without an atmosphere of rising consumer and business expectations. This represents the highest challenge to our political leadership. We can reach the Good Society within the limits of the system we cherish.

STATISTICAL
APPENDIX

The projection of potential output in future years is an enjoyable game at which any number can play. By varying our assumptions, we can forecast any desired estimate of employment and output for some specified future year. The arithmetic optimists, for example, have superimposed the dynamic forces of the postwar period upon the population structure and behavior patterns that will prevail over the decade of the 1970s.

Any such projection, however, must be based upon four crucial assumptions:

1. The size of the labor force;
2. The length of the workweek;
3. The improvement in output per man-hour; and
4. The definition of "full employment."

Once we have decided upon each of these assumptions, the calculation of the potential level of employment and the gross national product in the future becomes a simple matter of using the multiplication tables.

The size of the labor force is a function of both the number of people of working age and of the percentage of that group coming out to seek jobs. Here is how these data have changed during the postwar years:

	1947	1957	1960	1965
Total population (mils.)	144.1	172.0	180.7	194.6
% aged 14–64	68.5	63.0	61.2	61.9
Population aged 14–64 (mils.)	98.5	108.4	110.6	120.1
% in civilian labor force	61.2	62.5	64.0	62.8
Civilian labor force	60.2	67.9	70.6	75.6
% increase per annum		1.2	1.2	1.4

We can see from this table that the growth in the number of people of working age lagged far behind the rest of the population during the years 1947 to 1960, but that the maturing of the postwar baby crop was already making itself felt by 1965. The shortage in the number of people of working age after the war was offset in part by an increasing participation rate—that is, an increasing percentage of the people in those age groups came out to seek employment.

Most observers expect the participation rate to increase in the years to come, largely because of more women at work. Authoritative projections by both the National Industrial Conference Board and the National Planning

Association[*] are based upon this assumption. If we assume that the participation rate will rise to 64.5 percent in 1970 and to 65.5 percent in 1980, here is the size of the potential labor force in those years:

	1965	1970	1980
Total population (mils.)[*]	194.6	207.5	240.9
% aged 14–64	61.9	63.3	63.0
Population aged 14–64 (mils.)	120.1	131.1	150.7
% in civilian labor force	62.8	64.5	65.5
Civilian labor force (mils.)	75.6	85.0	99.0
% increase per annum		2.3	1.7

[*] Based on median Census Bureau projections.

This table shows that the labor force in the years ahead will be growing at a much faster rate than it grew from 1947 to 1965. The growth rate from 1965 to 1970 is somewhat overstated because the participation rate in 1965 was probably abnormally low.

The workweek is also generally expected to decline in the years ahead, as much due to longer vacations and increased holidays as to changes in the definition of the standard work week of forty hours. The workweek shrank 1.1 hours, or about 0.3 percent a year, from 1947 to 1960, although it then declined at a slightly slower rate from 1960 to 1965. Both the Conference Board and the National Planning Association expect the further decline

---

[*] See note 3 to Chapter 1.

to accelerate at first and then to slow down somewhat; thus, we may project a drop from 40.0 hours in 1965 to 39.0 hours in 1970 and 38.0 hours in 1980.

But how much will each worker produce during an hour's employment? The improvement in gross national product per man-hour has fluctuated widely in the postwar period, as the following table shows:

	1947	1957	1960	1965
Civilian employment (mils.)	57.8	65.0	66.7	72.1
Hours worked per week	41.5	41.0	40.4	40.0
Available man-hours (bils.)	124	138	139	150
Gross national production ($ bils.)*	344	502	542	676
GNP per man-hour ($)	2.77	3.63	3.90	4.50
% increase per annum		2.8	2.4	3.0

* In dollars of 1965 purchasing power.

The National Industrial Conference Board projects an increase in GNP per man-hour of a little less than three percent for the period from 1964 to 1975, but the 1965 annual report of the President's Council of Economic Advisors states that the long-term productivity trend is "slightly over three percent," while the National Planning Association expects an annual improvement of 3.3 percent from 1962 to 1975. Thus, we are hardly overstating the case of the arithmetic optimists if we project a rise in output per man-hour of 3.1 percent from 1965 to 1970 and 3.3 percent from 1970 to 1980. Based on a figure of

$4.50 for GNP per man-hour in 1965, this indicates a level of $5.21 for 1970 and $7.20 for 1980. This is, incidentally, a dramatic commentary on the economic power of the United States, for it suggests that output per man-hour will have doubled between 1957 and 1980.

We now have a projection for how many people will be seeking work, how many hours they will be working when they are employed, and how much they will be able to produce in each of those hours. How many jobs will we have to create if everyone who wants work is to be able to find it? Definitions of "full employment" are elusive, for it is physically impossible for *everyone* in the labor force to be employed: some duffers will inevitably be fired, some workers will quit jobs to seek others, some will be ill, and so on. Unemployment has seldom averaged much less than 4.0 percent of the labor force in this country. Although the first edition of this book set 3.5 percent unemployment as the practicable minimum, recent experience suggests that the figure of 4.0 percent is a more reasonable expectation.

In 1965, employment averaged 72.1 million out of a labor force of 75.6 million. Unemployment therefore ran around 3.5 million during the year, which meant an unemployment rate of 4.6 percent of the labor force. With the accelerated growth in the labor force coming from 1965 to 1970, the achievement of full employment by then will require a substantial increase in the number of available jobs, as the following table indicates:

	1960	1965	1970	1980
Civilian labor force (mils.)	70.6	75.6	85.0	99.0
% unemployed	5.6	4.6	4.0	4.0
Unemployment (mils.)	3.9	3.5	3.4	4.0
Civilian employment (mils.)	66.7	72.1	81.6	95.0
% increase per annum		1.7	2.5	2.0

Thus, in absolute terms, we will have to provide more than nine million jobs from 1965 to 1970 as compared with only 5.4 million new jobs that opened up from 1960 to 1965—when the unemployment rate was being sharply reduced. This is the steep requirement set by the enormous influx of young workers that our high postwar birth rates are now putting into the labor force. Although less intense a problem during the 1970s, the creation of enough jobs for full employment will still be a difficult task in that decade as well.

If we now put all of the assumptions together—the number of people at work, the length of the workweek, and output per man-hour—we can calculate the gross national product that we will be capable of turning out in future years. Remember that these are only calculations of capabilities rather than forecasts of things to come; they are merely a use of the multiplication tables rather than serious economic analysis. They are all expressed in dollars of 1965 purchasing power, so that price influences are eliminated and only physical changes in production and employment are reflected in them:

	1960	1965	1970	1975
Population 14–64 (mils.)	110.6	120.1	131.1	150.7
% in civilian labor force	64.0	62.8	64.5	65.5
Civilian labor force (mils.)	70.6	75.6	85.0	99.0
Civilian employment (mils.)	66.7	72.1	81.6	95.0
Weekly hours of work	40.4	40.0	39.0	38.0
Available man-hours ($)	139	150	165	187
GNP per man-hour ($)	3.90	4.50	5.21	7.20
Total GNP ($ bils.)	542	676	860	1350
% increase per annum		4.5	4.8	4.6

Given all of the underlying assumptions, then, this table shows that *we can provide jobs for all who seek them in future years only if the demand for goods and services can maintain the urgent upsweep that characterized the unusually prosperous years from 1960 to 1965—when government spending was rising and tax cuts were enacted at the same time.* In contrast, even the highly prosperous decade from 1947 to 1957 showed only 3.9 percent a year growth in gross national product in constant prices, while the slow-growth years from 1957 to 1960 showed an increase of only 2.6 percent a year. Hence, the accomplishments of the 1960 to 1965 period stand out in bold relief and the necessities of the coming fifteen years or so appear to loom large indeed.

What will be the consequences if the growth in demand is less than 4.6 percent or 4.8 percent a year? Assuming that the improvement in output per man-hour is the same as the rate that we have used in the calculations above, but that demand grows either at the relatively favorable 1947 to 1957 rate, say, 4.0 percent a year, or at the long-term historical rate of 3.0 percent a year, employment and unemployment levels would be as follows:

	1965	GNP Growth 4%		GNP Growth 3%	
	1965	**1970**	**1980**	**1970**	**1980**
Total GNP ($ bils.)	676	825	1220	785	1050
Civilian employment (mils.)	72.1	78.5	85.2	74.5	73.5
Unemployment (mils.)	3.5	6.5	13.8	10.5	25.5
% unemployed	4.6	7.6	14.0	12.3	25.8

The implications of this table are so clear that they require little comment. Even if the labor force has been over-stated in our assumptions, even if automation progresses more slowly, even if the workweek drops faster than we expect, we would appear to be headed for trouble unless the demand for goods and services does expand at a pace well above the rate that our long-run experience suggests is feasible.

Of course, output per man-hour does rise at a slower rate when output is rising slowly. Thus, we may ask what the level of employment would be under these more conservative assumptions of demand growth if output per man-hour rose at an annual rate of only 2.5 percent instead of better than 3.0 percent as assumed above. Here is what the projections would look like after this revision:

	1965	GNP Growth 4%		GNP Growth 3%	
		1970	1980	1970	1980
Total GNP ($ bils.)	676	825	1220	785	1050
Civilian employment (mils.)	72.1	80.2	94.5	78.0	82.0
Unemployment (mils.)	3.5	4.8	4.5	7.0	17.0
% unemployed	4.6	5.5	4.6	8.2	17.2

Thus, a somewhat slower rate of improvement in productivity could contribute importantly to holding down the level of unemployment as long as economic growth is still at an historically high level; we shall still have a heavy burden of unemployment under these circumstances if economic growth slows down to any noticeable extent. In any case, sacrifice of technological advancement would seem to be a poor way to solve our problems.

Other more desirable types of adjustment are possible, of course. Early retirement, more years of education, and changed attitudes toward work by women would reduce the participation rate and thus curtail the number of people seeking work. If we were willing to change our view of work in this manner so that the participation rate dropped instead of rising, this could make a significant difference. If the participation rate held to 62 percent of the people aged 14 to 64 instead of rising to 64.5 percent in 1970 and 65.5 percent in 1980, the 1970 labor force would shrink by nearly four million and the 1980 labor force would shrink by five million. A trend of this type could conceivably lead to labor shortages in 1970 and a greatly reduced burden of unemployment in 1980—although they would also have their costs in terms of goods and services that were never produced because of a smaller labor force.

ACKNOWLEDGMENTS

After many years of idle curiosity in reading other authors' acknowledgments, I have finally come to realize the full meaning of the contribution that one's friends can bring to a work of this sort. With the usual demurrers about all errors being of my own making, I must nevertheless admit freely and with pleasure that whatever merit this book may have has been provided in large measure by the unselfish and stimulating help of others.

My business associates, Linhart Stearns and Harold Edelstein, have given me the benefit of careful and critical readings of the manuscript, but, even more, many hours of pleasant discussion and argument with them have deepened and enriched my thinking on these subjects. Alan Sweezy, of the California Institute of Technology, gave me a large number of unusually valuable suggestions, especially in the earlier chapters of the book. My colleague at The New School for Social Research, David

Schwartzman, helped me think out some of the economic consequences of our population structure. John Heimann, of Smith, Barney, & Co., made an important contribution to the basic philosophy I have expressed in the last chapter. Hayden Smith, of Standard Oil Co. (N.J.), was helpful in working out part of the statistical analysis to which Gerhard Colm, of the National Planning Association, was also kind enough to give me the benefit of his assistance. My editor at Doubleday, Sam Vaughan, proved how one could be a firm friend and a stern critic at the same time.

Three people have earned a special measure of my gratitude: I can truly say that the book would never have been written without them. My teacher, Adolph Lowe, provided the essential philosophical and theoretical approach that shaped the ideas I have expressed. My friend, Robert L. Heilbroner, managed to combine an extraordinarily generous critical contribution with the warm enthusiasm and inspiration that all of us find so necessary in a task of this kind. The dedication to my wife was no casual choice: without her unfailing encouragement, good humor, and compassion this would have been a dismal and thankless business indeed.

NOTES

CHAPTER 1 The Arithmetic of Optimism

1. See Klein, L. R. and Kosobud, R. F., "Some Econometrics of Growth: Great Ratios of Economics," *Quarterly Journal of Economics,* Vol. LXXV, No. 2, May 1961 and also Hickman, B. G., *Investment Demand and U.S. Economic Growth,* Brookings Institution (Washington, D.C.: 1965).

2. The most striking aspect of this is the manner in which productivity responds to rapidly expanding demands. See Creamer, D., "Postwar Trends in the Relation of Capital to Output in Manufactures," *American Economic Review,* Vol. XLVIII, No. 2, May 1958. In general, however, shortages have never lasted more than a couple of years at most in the American economy.

3. See National Industrial Conference Board, *Economic Potentials of the United States in the Next Decade* (New York: 1965) and National Planning Association, *National Economic Projections to 1974* (Washington, D.C.: 1964).

4. Hickman, B. G., *op. cit.*

CHAPTER 2   The Burden of Government

1. Bator, F., *The Question of Government Spending,* Harper & Bros. (New York: 1960), pp. 21–22.

2. *The Congressional Record,* January 17, 1957, p. 695.

3. Transcript of news conference, the *New York Times,* January 15, 1959, p. 18.

4. Galbraith, J. K., *The Affluent Society,* Houghton-Mifflin (Boston: 1958), pp. 135, 261, and 267.

5. Quoted in *Business Week,* February 25, 1961, pp. 24–25.

6. Keynes, J. M., *The General Theory of Employment, Interest, and Money,* Harcourt, Brace (New York: 1936), pp. 129 and 131.

CHAPTER 3   The Fear of Taxes

1. See Hansen, A., *Economic Issues of the 1960's,* McGraw-Hill (New York: 1961), pp. 109–110.

2. Peacock, A. T. and Wiseman, J., "The Past and Future of Public Spending," *Lloyds Bank Review,* No. 60, April 1961.

3. Groves, H. M. and Kahn, C. H., "The Stability of State and Local Tax Yields," *American Economic Review,* Vol. 42, No. 1 (March 1952), p. 94. See also Lampman, R. J., "How Much Government Spending in the 1960's?" *The Quarterly Review of Economics and Business,* University of Illinois, Vol. 1, No. 1 (February 1961), p. 15, and Eckstein, O., *Trends in Public Expenditures in the Next Decade,* Committee for Economic Development (New York: 1959), pp. 43–46.

4. Liebenberg, M. and Fitzwilliams, J. M., "Size Distribution of Personal Incomes, 1957–60," *Survey of Current Business,* May 1961, p. 14.

5. Fitzwilliams, J. M., "Size Distribution of Personal Incomes, 1963, *Survey of Current Business,* April 1964, p. 8.

6. Ibid., p. 9, Table 11.

7. Committee for Economic Development, op. cit., pp. 11–12.

8. Fitzwilliams, J. M., op. cit., p. 9, Table 11.

9. From a study by the British National Institute of Economic and Social Research, cited in an article by Edwin L. Dale, Jr., the *New York Times,* March 22, 1961.

CHAPTER 4   The Uses of Government

1. Committee for Economic Development, *Growth and Taxes* (New York: 1961), p. 7.

2. Tawney, R. H., *Equality* (4th revised ed.), pp. 134–135, cited in Galbraith, J. K., *The Affluent Society,* Houghton-Mifflin (Boston: 1958), p. 251.

3. Tyson, R. C., speech before the Manufacturing Chemists Association, June 8, 1961.

4. Population Reference Bureau, *Demographic Factors in Community Health Planning,* Volume XVII, No. 1 (February 1961), p. 5.

5. Ibid., pp. 2–3.

6. Hagen, E. E., "Some Facts About Income Levels and Economic Growth," *Review of Economics and Statistics,* Vol. XLII, No. 1 (February 1960), Table 1.

7. Statement by Eugene R. Black, president of the International Bank for Reconstruction and Development, cited in the *New York Times,* April 25, 1961.

8. Hagen, op. cit., p. 64.

9. Population Reference Bureau, *Fertility Cult: U.S.A.,* Vol. XVI, No. 7 (October 1960), p. 141.

10. Quoted in the New York *World-Telegram & Sun,* April 4, 1961.

Chapter 6 The Economics of Democracy

1. I am grateful for this analysis to McConnell, C. R., "Social Imbalance: Where Do We Stand?" *University of Illinois Quarterly Review of Economics and Business,* Vol. I, No. 2, May 1961, pp. 17–19.

2. Wallich, H. C., *The Cost of Freedom*, Harper & Bros. (New York: 1960), pp. 57 and 71.

3. The *New York Times,* August 1, 1961.

INDEX

Advertising, 77

Affluent society, 11, 76–77

Antitrust prosecutions 107–108

Arithmetic optimism, 4, 8, 14–15, 121

Automation, 2, 15, 128

Bator, Francis, 18n

Birth rates:
  decline in, 6
  demand and, 14
  historical trends in, 6–8
  postwar, 126

Boondoggling, 81–82

Break, G. F., on taxation, 36

Business investment:
  determined by expectations, 13, 98–99
  for modernization, 9
  see also Expectations; Investment

Capital gains, 42

Capital goods, increase in, 9–10

Capitalism:
  characteristics of, 116
  increase in, 9–10
  meaning of, 101–104

Change:
  fear of, 113–114
  persistence of, 5–7
  see also Technological change

City planning, 70

Colm, Gerhard, 132

Committee on Economic Development:
  on growth of federal expenditures, 57–58, 62
  on tax on high incomes, 44

Community:
  public services and the, 59–64
  taxation as a "loss" to the, 64–65

Competition, foreign, 49
Conservatives:
  defense spending and,
    112–114
  opposed to government
    spending, 63–65
Consumer demand. *See*
  Demand
Consumer spending:
  inflation and, 86n, 87n
  significance of, 10, 12–14
  see also Demand
Consumer surplus, 62n
Corporate taxes:
  characteristics of, 41
  prices and, 49
Council of Economic Advisors,
  President's, 124

Defense spending:
  characteristics of, 23–26
  epitomizes maintenance of
    status quo, 112–114
  and expansion of capacity,
    91–92
Demand:
  business investment and,
    13–14
  consumer surplus, 62n
  economic growth, 5
  expansion in, 16
  growth in, 127–128
  outlook for, 12
  postwar, 14–15
  productivity and, 11
  transfer payments and, 21–22
  see also Consumer spending

Democracy:
  centralized *vs.* free economy
    in, 104–111
  government spending in,
    28–31
  public services in, 59–63
Depreciation. *See* Taxes
Depression. *See* Great
  Depression
Deval, Jacques, on destiny, 78

Economic freedom, 109–111
Economic man, 66
Economics, importance of
  demand in, 5
Economies:
  dynamic, 31–34
  free enterprise, 14
  free *vs.* centralized, 104–109
  Soviet *vs.* U.S., 114–117
  see also Change
Edelstein, Harold, 131
Education, as public service, 59,
  68, 129
Eisenhower, Dwight D., on
  government spending,
  28–29
Employee compensation. *See*
  Wages
Employment:
  forecasting, 121–122, 125–128
  see also Full employment;
    Labor force;
    Unemployment
Europe:
  free economies in, 105
  taxation and growth in, 54

Index

Expectations, business activities and, 54, 98–99

Exports, helped by foreign aid, 74–75

Featherbedding, 82

Forecasts:
crucial assumption in, 10
employment, 121–122, 125–128
fallacies of, 2
output, potential, 121
unemployment, 125–126

Foreign aid:
foreign trade and, 73–74
impact of, 70–76

Foreign competition, taxes and, 49

Free enterprise economy:
characteristics of, 14, 51, 54, 106–111
Soviet economy *vs.*, 114–117

Full employment:
characteristics of, 4–5, 126
definition of, 121, 125
inflation and, 87–88, 90–91
prerequisites for, 119
tax cuts and, 47

Galbraith, John Kenneth:
economic theory, 76–77
on government spending, 29

Government intervention:
government regulation distinct from government spending, 107–108
in market place, 101–109

Government spending:
attitudes toward, current, 18–19
as choice instead of unemployment, 32, 79, 97
compensatory, 28
expectations and, 98–99
government regulation independent from, 108
as inadequate, 81, 97
as inflationary, 81–93
in Keynesian economics, 102
need for, 63–73
nondefense outlays relatively stable, 24–27
on per capita basis has shown tendency to decline, 23–24
possible frightening of businessmen by, 98–100
prejudice against, 19–20, 25, 27–30, 62–64, 79–80, 98–99, 104–105, 118–119
"price" of public services, 58–64
as protection of our freedoms, 118
ratio of GNP of, 24
should decline relatively as income rises, 57
stimulation of growth by, 5, 31–35, 44–46, 84, 96–97
structural unemployment and, 93–96
two categories of, 20–21
as wasteful, 81–84, 97

Government spending
  (*Continued*)
  when opponents of spending
    have a strong case, 109
  whether excessive, 22–35
  see also Defense spending;
    Taxes
Great Depression, 3, 6, 13,
  103, 116
Gross national product (GNP):
  calculation of, 122, 125–127
  government sector and,
    21, 24
  improvement in, 123
  in other countries, 71
  percentage devoted to
    foreign aid, 73n
  taxation rises as GNP rises,
    40–43, 48
  see also Output
Growth, economic, stimulated
  by government, 5, 9, 97

Hauser, Philip M., on city
  planning, 69
Heilbroner, Robert L., xv, 132
Heimann, John, 132
Household formation, 8
Housing, subsidization of,
  61–62, 104
Humphrey, George, on govern-
  ment spending, 27–28

Incentives, taxation and,
  20–22, 36, 50–54. *See also*
  Investment

Income:
  high incomes not effectively
    taxed, 40–45, 49, 66
  personal, 3
India, investment required in,
  71–72
Inflation:
  consumer spending and,
    86n, 87n
  defined, 83–84
  demand and, 85–86
  demand-pull and cost-push
    theories of, 85–86
  government spending and,
    23, 81–93
  of 1946–1948, 3
  wage-price spiral in, 9
  war and, 88–89
Investment:
  government spending and,
    50–52
  inflation and, 88, 93
  in postwar years, 50–55
  see also Business investment;
    Incentives
Isaacs, Reginald, on city
  planning, 69–70

Kahn, Harry C., 44n
Keynes, John Maynard:
  on business, 98
  on government spending, 19,
    32, 103
Klipper, Miriam Z.,
  xxvi
Korean War, 15, 24, 50

Index

Labor force:
  government spending and,
    33–34, 93–96
  growth in, 4, 7, 125
  increase in, 8
  productivity and, 17
  shortage of, 6, 10, 17, 128
  significance of, 128
  size of, 17, 121–123
  surplus of, 17
  women in, 11
  see also Employment; Wages
Labor-saving machinery, 93.
    See also Automation;
    Technological change
Labor unions:
  cost-push inflation and, 85
  monopoly in, 85
  overemployment in, 82
Lowe, Adolph, 132
Lusk, Robert E., on advertising,
    76–77

Markets, saturated, 70
Marriage. See Birth rates
Monopoly, in labor
    unions, 85

National Bureau of Economic
    Research, 44n
National Industrial Conference
    Board, 12–13, 122, 124
National Planning
    Association:
  on city planning, 69n
  functions of, 13, 122–124

Obsolescence:
  impact of, 93
  planned, 81–83
Optimism, arithmetic of, 4, 8,
    14–15
Output, forecast for 1970s,
    10–11. See also Gross
    national product (GNP);
    Overemployment;
    Productivity
Overemployment, 82

Peacock, Alan T., on taxation,
    38–39
Pessimism, arithmetic of,
    15. See also Optimism,
    arithmetic of
Planned economy. See
    Socialism
Population. See Birth rates;
    City planning; Labor force
Postal service, 60–61
Postwar years:
  characteristics of, 3, 6
  consumer demand during,
    12–15
  economic incentive
    during, 50
  increase in productivity
    during, 15
  output and productivity
    during, 14–15
Poverty, 2, 35, 52–53, 66, 81, 108
Price level:
  corporate income taxes
    and, 50

Price level (*Continued*)
government spending and,
23–24
see also Inflation
Private sector:
criticisms of public sector
apply also to, 81–82
demands of, 16
Productivity (output per
man-hour):
determined by demand for
and supply of labor, 11
forecasting the amount of,
121, 126
improvement in, 15, 45, 121,
127–128
technological unemployment
and, 15
Profit margins:
relationship of high profits to
high investment, 52
taxes and, 49–50
Public sector:
legitimate activities of,
59–64
sorely lacking in necessities,
66–69
see also Government spending

Railroads, subsidization of, 61
Retirement, early, 129
Roosevelt, Franklin D., on
needless self-interest, 56

Schwartzmann, David, 132
Smith, Hayden, 132
Social balance, 76

Socialism:
characteristics of, 63, 105
distinction between
American economy and,
105–107
Social status:
defense spending and,
112–114
economic freedom and, 111n
Soviet Union, economic goals
of, 114–117
Stearns, Linhart, 131
Sweezy, Alan, 131

Tawney, R. H., on collective
provision for needs,
63–64
Taxes:
on capital gains, 42
corporate, 41, 49
economic incentives and, 19,
21, 36, 50–54
effect of possible reduction
in, 46–50
future possible increase in,
39–42
on income, 42–45, 65
inflation and, 87
as "loss" to community,
64–65
resistance to, 36–40, 44–45
risk and, 54
separation of taxation and
public spending decisions,
99–100
summary of case against high
taxation, 56–57

wages and, 52–53
see also Government
spending
Technological change
impact of, 11, 14, 51, 93,
96, 129
unemployment and, 15
Tobin, James, on cynicism
toward democracy, 30–31
Tourism, 76
Transfer payments, 20–22
Tuke, Anthony, 1
Tyson, Robert C., on government spending, 65

Underdeveloped countries,
economic problems,
71–72, 91. *See also*
Foreign aid
Unemployment:
birth rates and, 6–8
as choice instead of government spending, 31–32,
79, 96
expected increase in
1960s, 116
forecasting, amount of,
124–127
"freedom" of, 110–111
inflation and, 86–87, 90, 94
reduced burden of, 128–129
significance of, 8, 15–16

structural *vs.* cyclical, 93–96
technological, 15
Unions. *See* Labor unions
United States Steel
Corporation, 65
Urban problems, 69

Vaughan, Sam, 132

Wage-price spiral. *See* Inflation
Wages (employee
compensation):
taxes and, 52–53
wastefulness in, 81
Wallich, Henry, on centralized
vs. free economy, 105
War, inflation and, 88–89
Ward, Artemus, 18
Waste, in both public and
private sectors, 79–82, 97
West Germany, taxation and
growth in, 54
Wiseman, Jack, on taxation,
38–39
Workers. *See* Employment;
Labor force; Productivity;
Unemployment
Work week:
effect on reduction in, 16
length of, 121, 123, 126–128
World War II. *See* Postwar
years